Anna Mazzanti

THE ART OF FLORENCE

IN ITS GREAT MUSEUMS

BECOCCI
SCALA

CONTENTS

A tour that passes through the greatest museums in Florence brings the visitor into contact with so many masterpieces of Western art, of such quality and in so rapid succession, as to trigger feelings of bewilderment and stupor: a reaction now known by the name of the "Stendhal Syndrome." In fact the museums of Florence, under the ownership and management of a variety of bodies – the State, the Municipality, the Florentine Curia, and others – contain a vast and priceless heritage: the collections of the Medici dynasty, and of their successors as grand dukes of Tuscany, the house of Lorraine; the sacred works of art produced for the cathedral and the churches of the great religious orders; the fruit of public commissions by the Signoria and the grand dukes; and finally works that used to belong to noble and bourgeois families, in an unbroken tradition of artistic patronage. A guide to this fascinating and complex world is essential, whether one wishes to make the most of a stay in the city, however long or short, a series of visits, or even just one, to a particular museum chosen for whatever reason. The function of an intelligent and practical guidebook, like this one, is to help visitors, with balanced suggestions, to make their way from one museum to another, from one room to another, from one work to another, without losing sight of the history and the development of art in Florentine culture as a whole. How can one fail, in fact, to linger in front of masterpieces like Botticelli's Primavera in the Galleria degli Uffizi or Michelangelo's David in the Galleria dell'Accademia, capable by themselves of drawing large numbers of people from all over the world? It is true that, in this age of all-pervading and instant communications, their images (along with those of a few other works of art of universal value) now travel right around the world, in a myriad of forms and for a myriad of purposes. Yet I think that it is equally true, however paradoxical it may seem, that the greater the number of illustrations, copies, reproductions in books or on calendars, postcards, objects, CD-ROMs, and other forms in which people come into indirect contact with the work, the greater is the value of the original as an object of veneration. And to see it in the flesh, so to speak, taking away a personal memory, is worth going through all the rituals of a modern pilgrimage.

Thus certain visits and certain stops are indispensable. And confirmation of this is provided in the guide, which includes the city's most representative museums and, within them, the pictures, statues, and frescoes without which a visit to the city by a non-Florentine or non-Italian would perhaps lose its sense.

In parallel to this obligatory route, however, the author provides visitors with all the indications they need to follow another itinerary of great interest, one that will help them to comprehend the settings themselves (outstanding among them, for their sheer quantity, the monastic quarters of San Marco, the Grand Ducal Apartments of Palazzo Vecchio, the Quartiere Planetario in Palazzo Pitti) along with a broader group of works of art. Among them can be found a carefully selected range of the applied arts, which, in a museum like the Bargello for instance, are of unquestionable significance.

The care lavished on the illustrations, as is the publisher's tradition, makes this guidebook an excellent traveling companion. One that is worth consulting before you make a move, in order to plan an itinerary; during the visits themselves, for a full and satisfying comprehension of what you see; and on your return, to evoke and fix in the memory a personal store of images, an immaterial but priceless treasure to be kept among your most precious memories.

Cristina Acidini Luchinat
Deputy Head of the Fine Art and Monuments Service

GALLERIA DEGLI
UFFIZI

The oldest museum collection in the world can also lay claim to preeminence in the quality of the works it contains, boasting some of the greatest masterpieces of the Florentine Renaissance. These make it one of the most popular of all galleries, visited by large numbers of the public and scholars alike. But the Uffizi gallery is also unique from the architectural point of view: in fact it is laid out in the shape of a "U" with very long arms, in a spectacular location between Piazza della Signoria and the river. The windows of its three corridors offer wonderful views of the heart of the city, and visitors to the museum are exposed to a constant dialogue between the interior and the surrounding architecture and landscape.

The Uffizi were designed by Giorgio Vasari, the architect, painter, and writer – an "all-round" artist in the true spirit of his time – who was much admired by Cosimo I. In 1559 the latter commissioned this building from him as a seat for the principal magistracies (the word *uffizi* means "offices") of the duchy of Tuscany. The passage that runs across the Ponte Vecchio and connects the building to Palazzo Pitti was Cosimo's idea too. Later known as the Corridoio Vasariano, it was built by the architect in the space of just

five months (1565) and inaugurated on the occasion of the marriage of Cosimo's son Francesco to Joan of Austria. It was the duke's intention that this unusual construction should serve as a link between the center of political life, represented by Palazzo Vecchio – connected to the Uffizi by a simple bridge over the street –, and the family residence of Palazzo Pitti. The aim was to create a means of communication that would allow him to move around quickly and safely without ever emerging into the open air.

It was not until later (1581), however, after the completion of the building by Bernardo Buontalenti, that Grand Duke Francesco I chose to house a large part of the Medici family's remarkable collections of art on the upper floor. The Tribuna, in particular, a curious octagonal structure located in the east wing and fruit of the

marriage between Francesco I's cultural eclecticism and Buontalenti's creative genius, took the form of a chamber of "wonders," a showcase for the cream of the family collections.

At the outset, though, the Galleria degli Uffizi did not have the predominant character of an art gallery that it was to assume later on, starting with the first changes carried out by the Lorraine family and leading up to the more thorough reorganization following the unification of the country. Rather it was a more "general" museum, housing a wide variety of testimonies to human ingenuity. In fact the gallery had displays of scientific instruments, ancient and modern weapons, classical bronzes, and astronomical instruments, and much space and energy was devoted to the collection of ancient art, some examples of which can still be seen

in the entrance hall and along the three corridors. The western corridor, which now provides access to the rooms devoted to painting from the sixteenth to the eighteenth century, was originally occupied by craft workshops and the "Fonde-

The Uffizi, view of the facade from the river Arno

Pages 4-5:
Giuseppe Zocchi
View of the Uffizi from the River Arno
Museo di Firenze com'era

The Corridoio Vasariano on the Ponte Vecchio

Left:
The Uffizi showing the characteristic "U" shape of the building

The Corridoio Vasariano after its recent renovation

ria," where perfumes were distilled and experiments carried out with medicines and poisons. It terminated in a hanging garden set on top of the Loggia dei Lanzi, which was used for the musical pastimes of the grand ducal family and as a privi-

leged vantage point from which to watch celebrations in the square. Each generation of the Medici family added to the collections. Particular mention should be made of the contribution of Ferdinando II, who, through the inheritance of his

wife Vittoria della Rovere, was able to add masterpieces by Titian, Raphael, and Piero della Francesca. But the most extraordinary collector of all was Cardinal Leopoldo, who was responsible for the creation of the nuclei of three of the specific groups of works that help to make the Uffizi such a unique museum: the miniature portraits (of which there are around 1300 today); the systematic collection of drawings by old and modern masters that lies at the origin of the famous Gabinetto di Disegni e Stampe, which has grown in prestige and size over time to its present total of 110,000 folios; and the collection of self-portraits by painters of many nationalities, now much enlarged and hung along the walls of the Corridoio Vasariano until such time as they are provided with a more suitable location by the reorganization of the museum that is currently under way.

With the death of the last Medici grand duke, in 1737, and the subsequent passage of the grand duchy of Tuscany to the

Lorraine family, the collections ran the risk of dispersion or transfer. In a providential and farsighted decision, however, the last descendant of the Medici, Electress Palatine Anna Maria Ludovica, ceded (in 1737) the entire collection of art to the house of Lorraine on condition that it should be kept in Florence "*in perpetuo.*" In any case the experience of rule by the new grand dukes was generally a positive

one, and while they did not have the same inclination to patronage as the Medici, it remains a fact that they continued to enrich the collections, in particular with works by the "primitives." They were favored in this by the policy of suppression of religious bodies. Pietro Leopoldo also promoted the reorganization of the collections and the transfer of specific groups of exhibits from the gallery to special museums.

In more recent times the Uffizi have been subjected to numerous interventions of a museological character: the incorporation of the former church of San Pier Scheraggio, which now forms the first stage on the tour of the museum; the restructuring of the rooms devoted to the Middle Ages and the early Renaissance; the reorganization and very recent renovation of the Corridoio Vasariano; and the faithful

restoration of the Tribuna, to mention just a few of the most important. Yet the grave problem of the lack of suitable exhibition spaces remains unresolved, and a solution will have to be found if the museum is to cope with the slow but constant increase in the number of works on the one hand, and the spectacular rise in the number of visitors, now over ten times larger than it was just a few decades ago. The answer to this problem should lie in the creation of the "Grandi Uffizi," a plan that is half a century old but which now seems to have

entered a more dynamic phase. This would make it possible to use the two upper floors of the building for the art gallery, and the ground floor for all those services necessary to the functioning of such a large museum. A sad interruption to the plans of expansion and to the activity of the gallery itself came with the dynamite attack on via dei Georgofili (May 27, 1993), which suddenly thrust the Uffizi into the headlines. The explosion did irreparable damage to three paintings and injured another 173 pictures and fifty sculptures to the point where they required restoration. But the encouraging response shown by the museum's staff, the intense program of restoration carried out over an extremely limited space of time, which in many cases has provided an opportunity for new advances in methodology and interpretation, and the renovation of the western corridor – the one affected by the explosion – all represent positive signs for the future.

Above left:
view of the first corridor

right:
the Tribuna

The Hall of Thirteenth-Century Painting

Andrea del Castagno (Castagno, Mugello, ca. 1421 – Florence 1457)
■ *The Cumaean Sibyl*
Church of San Pier Scheraggio
detached fresco transferred onto canvas, 250x154 cm
This figure of a sibyl is part of a cycle of frescoes depicting illustrious men and woman that the artist painted around 1450 in the loggia of Villa Carducci at Legnaia (in the vicinity of Florence). Today it is on show in this first and highly unusual section of the gallery: the nave of the old church of San Pier Scheraggio which was incorporated into the museum several decades ago. The source of iconographic inspiration for the cycle should be sought in the medieval tradition of representing well-known personages to be held up as examples of good civil and moral conduct. Andrea del Castagno chose six men who played a significant role in the history and culture of Florence (Dante, Boccaccio, Petrarch, and three *condottieri*, Pippo Spano, Farinata degli Uberti, and Niccolò Acciaioli) and three famous women of antiquity (Esther, queen of the Persians, Tomyris, queen of the Scythians, and the Cumaean Sibyl). The solid and imposing appearance of the figures is reminiscent of Piero della Francesca and Masaccio.

Cimabue (recorded 1272 – 1302)
■ *Santa Trinita Madonna*
Room 2
panel, 425x243 cm
This is the oldest of the great *Maestà* that dominate the Sala del Duegento and, along with the other two masterpieces, constitutes a sort of solemn preamble to the chronological tour of the gallery and an introduction to the characteristics of modern Italian art.
We know little of the history of this recently restored (1992) picture, just as the life and activity of its author remains largely obscure. But the high quality of the work is proof that

he had already attained an artistic maturity, in which the elegant and harmonious arrangement of the angels and the graphic depiction of the drapery derived from an older tradition are combined with more modern solutions. The throne, for example, where an attempt has been made to create an impression of spatial depth, or the more markedly sculptural effect of the sacred group, still composed according to traditional criteria of solemnity but also showing signs, in the tenderness of the Virgin's expression as she gazes at the Child, of a new sensibility. Among the many different dates assigned to the work by art historians, the most widely accepted view is that it was painted in the 1380-90s, around the time of the frescoes for the basilica of San Francesco in Assisi.

Duccio di Buoninsegna
(Siena ca. 1255 – 1318/19)
■ *Rucellai Madonna*
Room 2
panel, 450x290 cm
Commissioned in 1285 by the Compagnia dei Laudesi of the Florentine church of Santa Maria Novella, Duccio's celebrated altarpiece takes its name from the Rucellai Chapel where it was housed for over three centuries before entering the Uffizi, in 1948. Long attributed to Cimabue on the basis of claims made by fourteenth-

century sources, which were later repeated by Vasari, it was not assigned to Duccio until the beginning of the twentieth century. However the affinities with Cimabue's *Maestà*, now in the Louvre, are undeniable and this picture was undoubtedly his source of inspiration. Yet here the young Duccio shows that he was able to enrich the heritage of tradition with his own, more personal language, in which the stylistic delicacies of the Gothic style that were later to become a fixed trait of Sienese painting put in their first appearance: the refinement of color, the elegant and supple lines – evident in the sinuous border of the Virgin's cloak –, the sumptuous drapery of Northern European derivation, and the complex structure of the throne. All characteristics that have been brought fully to light by the restoration of 1988-89.

Giotto (Vespignano, Vicchio di Mugello, 1267 – Florence 1337)
■ *Ognissanti Madonna*
Room 2
panel, 325x204 cm
A masterpiece by Giotto that can now be admired, after its restoration (1990-91), in all its majesty of form and brilliance of color, it was painted around 1310 for the Humiliati friars of Ognissanti, the Florentine church in which it hung for five centuries.
Though set against an abstract gold ground like the nearby *Maestà* of Cimabue and Duccio, the plastic definition of the figures and the construction of space to create an illusion of depth are indicative of a distance much greater than the gap of a few decades that separates the pictures. The Virgin above

all, so different from the transcendental Madonnas of the thirteenth century, with her serene expression and gentle hint of a smile and the solid construction of her forms, suggests a totally new interest in realism. Thanks to the restoration and the studies connected with it, new hypotheses have been put forward about the original location of the painting – always believed to have been the high altar of the church of Ognissanti – and the iconographic program, rich in references and symbols, that the artist followed.

Simone Martini (Siena ca. 1284 – ca. 1348) and **Lippo Memmi** (Siena, recorded 1317 – 1347)
■ *Annunciation and Saints*
Room 3
panel, 184x210 cm
One of the most significant works from the Sienese school of the fourteenth century, it comes from the altar of the chapel of Sant'Ansano in Siena Cathedral, for which it was painted in 1333. It represents a continuation of the Sienese tradition with its precious colors and supple and elegant treatment of anatomy inspired by Gothic art from the other side of the Alps. It was painted by Simone Martini, the famous author of the *Maestà* in the Palazzo Pubblico of Siena, together with his brother-in-law Lippo Memmi. The paternity of the work is recorded in the inscription on the nineteenth-century frame that surrounds it, but it is fairly difficult to distinguish the contributions of the two artists in the absence of documentary evidence. On the basis of apparent differences in style, the wings – *Saint Ansano*, titular of the chapel from which the picture comes, and perhaps *Saint Margaret* – are ascribed to Memmi, while the beautiful central scene of the *Annunciation*, with the elegant figure of the frightened Virgin set alongside the angel, who is represented with extraordinary technical skill, is considered one of Simone's most mature achievements. The prevalent view among critics today, however, is that the collaboration between the two artists was too close to permit any clear distinction of their roles.

Ambrogio Lorenzetti
(Siena 1285 – ca. 1348)
■ *Presentation in the Temple*
Room 3
panel, 257x168 cm

Along with Simone Martini and Lippo
Memmi's *Annunciation*, this picture was part
of a cycle devoted to the Madonna in Siena
Cathedral, which had begun with Duccio's
great *Maestà* (Siena, Museo dell'Opera
Metropolitana) for the high altar. Ambrogio's
Presentation, was painted, by 1342 at the
latest, for the altar of San Crescenzio, from
which it was removed in the mid seventeenth
century. It is a work from the artist's full
maturity, painted around the same time as his
celebrated frescoes in Siena's Palazzo Pubblico
– one of the most significant mural
decorations of the fourteenth century –
shortly before he fell victim to the terrible
outbreak of plague in 1348. This picture too
quickly achieved great fame and was
frequently examined and imitated by later
artists.

A comparison with Simone's work
immediately reveals a very different approach
to the construction of form and,
notwithstanding the great richness of color
revealed by the restoration carried out a
decade ago, the composition is sustained by a

solidity and concreteness that shows the influence of Giotto's innovations. The human figures have proportions that are naturalistically in keeping with the elaborate and carefully studied architectural interior for which the painting is famous.

Giottino (Florence 1320/30 – post 1369)
■ *Pietà*
Room 4
panel, 195x134 cm
Originally in the Florentine church of San Remigio, for which it was painted around 1360-65, it is one of the most elegant pictures of the fourteenth century, attributed to this artist who is still shrouded in mystery.
The work displays stylistic features that set it apart from the Florentine tradition and that can be traced instead to the Lombard school (with which the painter may have come into contact through his father Stefano, who emigrated to Milan, or through the work of Giovanni da Milano in Florence): the elegant elongation of the bodies, the restrained sense of participation in the sacred drama where elegiac tones prevail over tragic ones, and the precise touches of realism, such as the bloodstain on the modern garment worn by the client, led onto the scene by St. Remigio.

Gentile da Fabriano
(Fabriano ca. 1370 – Rome 1427)
■ *Adoration of the Magi*
Room 5/6
panel, 300x282 cm
This large panel by Gentile perhaps provides a better example than any other of the style and sensibility of flamboyant Gothic, to which one whole room of the gallery is devoted: a current in painting that tended to maintain solid ties with the Gothic tradition but within a frame of reference that had been changed forever by the new ideas of Humanism.

The *Adoration*, we are informed by the inscription on the panel itself, was painted in May 1423 for the wealthy Florentine merchant, Palla di Noferi Strozzi, who placed it in his family chapel in Santa Trinita.

The atmosphere is as unreal as a courtly fable, and in the crowded retinue of the Three Kings the artist has given free rein to his imagination, portraying sumptuous garments decorated in relief with gold paste, along with exotic animals and hunting scenes.

Although Gentile's "old-fashioned" style deliberately ignores the most recent advances in the use of perspective for the construction of the scene, the altarpiece exercised a great influence on Florentine artists, and even some forty years later Benozzo Gozzoli took some of the ideas for his *Journey of the Magi* in the chapel of Palazzo Medici from the painting.

Piero della Francesca

(Borgo San Sepolcro 1410/20 – 1492)

■ *Federico da Montefeltro and Battista Sforza*
Room 7

panels, 47x33 cm (each)

These regal portraits of the duke and duchess
of Urbino, painted in profile in keeping with
the tradition of the medal portrait and with
representations of their allegorical triumphs set
on the back, entered the Medici collections as
part of the substantial inheritance of Vittoria
della Rovere. They were painted around 1465,
at a time when artists of great ability were
working at the court of Urbino and the
presence of many Flemish pictures allowed
him to make comparisons with the Northern
European school of painting. In fact the realistic
and painstaking attention to detail with which
the artist depicts Federico's face or the jewelry
and hairstyle of Battista are typical of the
Flemish manner, but infused with a new spirit
that goes beyond mere description. The way in
which he manages to make the two faces in
the foreground blend in with the beautiful
landscape in the background despite the lack of
any linking element is extremely impressive.

Filippo Lippi

(Florence ca. 1406 – Spoleto 1469)

■ *Madonna and Child with Two Angels*
Room 8

panel, 95x62 cm

The Galleria degli Uffizi houses a substantial
number of works by this indefatigable and
eccentric artist, a Carmelite friar who led a
dissolute life but also played a prominent role
in the fifteenth-century renewal of art.
They are located in a special room named
after him. Unquestionably the most celebrated
of them is this *Madonna and Child with Two
Angels*, a work from the latter part of his career
(1455-1466) in which it is possible to discern
the influence of contemporary sculpture, from
Luca della Robbia to Donatello, while the
airiness of the landscape and the curious
conformation of the rocks offer foretastes of
Leonardo.
Typical of Lippi's style, on the other hand, are
the faces of the angels, with their chubby
features and air of the "common folk," and the
delicacy of the drawing in the figure of the
Virgin, which was to have a great influence on
the young Botticelli.

Tommaso di Cristoforo Fini, called **Masolino** (San Giovanni Valdarno 1383? – 1440) and **Tommaso di Ser Giovanni**, called **Masaccio** (San Giovanni Valdarno 1401 – Rome 1428)
■ *Madonna and Child with Saint Ann*
Room 7
panel, 175x103 cm
Hung in a room of small size but one that holds an extremely significant place in the tour of the Uffizi, the *Madonna and Child with Saint Ann* marks, along with the other masterpieces located here, a crucial point in the transition from a still Gothic style to fully Renaissance forms of expression.
The work is a collaboration between Masolino and Masaccio, the first fruit of an artistic partnership that was to continue in the frescoes of the Brancacci Chapel and the *Santa Maria Maggiore Polyptych* in Rome (part now lost and part split up among various museums). It was almost certainly painted between 1424 and 1425.
In the now almost unanimously accepted view of a celebrated mid-century art historian, Roberto Longhi, the figure of St. Ann and the

angels – with the exception of the one dressed in green at top right – are by Masolino, the older artist who was still intent on producing a suffuse and graceful pictorial composition, while the Virgin and Child, with their sound handling of perspective and sculptural forms, are the work of Masaccio.

Paolo Uccello
(Pratovecchio, Arezzo, 1397 – Firenze 1475)
■ *The Battle of San Romano*
Room 7
panel, 182x220 cm
According to the inventory of Lorenzo the Magnificent's furnishings, this picture, along with two others of the same subject, used to decorate the walls of his personal chamber on the ground floor of the great palace on via Larga (now via Cavour). The three panels formed a sort of triptych commemorating the battle of San Romano on June 1, 1432, at which the Florentines defeated the Sienese. The painting in the Uffizi depicts the episode of the unhorsing of Bernardino della Ciarda by Niccolò da Tolentino, the *condottiere* who was also portrayed by Andrea del Castagno on a wall of the cathedral of Santa Maria del Fiore.
The subject provided this imaginative and original painter, whom Vasari described as "obsessed with perspective," with an opportunity to carry out experiments that

induced him to transform the knights and horses in the foreground into geometric figures, exercises particularly well-suited to the *mazzocchio*, the peculiar Renaissance headgear resembling a multifaceted cake. The beautiful landscape in the background, with scenes of hunting and grape picking, reveals the painter's Gothic origins and recalls the atmosphere created by the illuminations of the Limbourg brothers. But the unreal colors of the lances raised against the sky – set alongside the armor of the knights, once covered with silver leaf – bestow almost metaphysical accents of unusual modernity on the scene.

button of a cope. This may be an allusion to the Pollaiolo brothers' activity as goldsmiths. But the greatest merit of the cleaning has been its rejuvenation of the beautiful, glowing colors, the refined fabrics embellished with jewels, and the limpid stretch of landscape, confirming the preeminent role of Antonio, who must have been responsible for the composition of the altarpiece and much of its execution.

Sandro Filipepi, called **Botticelli**
(Florence 1445 – 1510)
■ *La Primavera*
Room 10/14
panel, 203x314 cm
This is perhaps the most famous of the whole group of splendid works by Botticelli in the Uffizi. It was painted for Lorenzo di Pierfrancesco de' Medici, who must have kept it for a long time in the palace on via Larga, and then in the Villa di Castello, where Vasari records its presence.
The difficulty of identifying the subject depicted has led to a vast number of iconographic interpretations, but the most likely is that it represents the realm of Venus. The many literary sources on which Botticelli appears to have drawn, from the *Stanzas* of the poet Politian to the neoplatonic philosophical

Antonio Benci, called **Pollaiolo** (Florence ca. 1431 – Rome 1498) and **Piero Benci**, called **Pollaiolo** (Florence ca. 1441 – Rome 1496)
■ *Saints James, Vincent, and Eustace*
Room 9
panel, 172x179 cm
This elegant altarpiece can still be admired in its original location by visiting the chapel of the Cardinal of Portugal in the church of San Miniato al Monte, where its place on the altar has been taken by a nineteenth-century copy. The purpose for which the picture was painted is recalled in the saints portrayed: James (in the middle), Vincent (on the left), and Eustace, all linked in some way to the cardinal to whom the chapel is dedicated, Jacobus of Lusitania.
It is worth noting the way that the original frame is perfectly in keeping with the colored flooring and the balustrade behind the saints, an example of the great skill attained by the

Florentine craft workshops of the Renaissance. The recent restoration has brought to light the cardinal's elegant coat of arms, inserted in the decoration of the frame in the form of the

theories of Marsilio Ficino, and the references to the broad range of classical authors who were read at the court of Lorenzo the Magnificent, including Lucretius, Horace, and Ovid, make it a wonderful example of the culture that held sway in the Medicean circles of the late fifteenth century.

The most convincing interpretation of the painting starts from the right, from the figure of Zephyr who unites with the nymph Chloris to create Flora, goddess of the spring, represented as a figure decked with flowers. In the middle of the picture Venus is crowned by the flying figure of the blindfolded Cupid, representing blind love, in the act of loosing an arrow at the group of the three Graces, who are dancing in a ring. Their union is a symbol of perfection and the agility of their movements combined with the lightness of their clothing create an impression of freedom in the Humanistic sense. The figure on the left dispersing the clouds with a staff – perhaps a citation of Verrocchio's *David*, now in the Bargello – represents Mercury, i.e. reason and intelligence. So this picture represents a sort of itinerary of the sublimation of earthly and instinctive love (Zephyr-Chloris) to the

spiritual (Graces) and intellectual spheres (Mercury).

Other interpretations, however, are linked to the symbolic meanings of the flowers (periwinkles, cornflowers, violets) scattered over the meadow – a true herbal collection – and the presence of mythological figures alluding to conjugal love, suggesting that the picture was painted to celebrate the marriage of Lorenzo di Pierfrancesco de' Medici to Semiramide d'Appiano.

Sandro Botticelli
■ *The Birth of Venus*
Room 10/14
canvas, 172x278 cm

It is immediately apparent that this second masterpiece by Botticelli is a product of the same refined cultural climate that gave rise to the *Primavera*. In Vasari's time it too was located in the Villa di Castello, although we do not know who commissioned the painting. It may have been the same man for whom the *Primavera* was painted: Lorenzo di Pierfrancesco de' Medici. Here too we find references to classical literature, and scholars

have linked the *Venus* to Homer's *Hymn to Venus*, Ovid's love poetry, and above all Politian's *Stanzas*. In fact Botticelli's painting almost seems to be a translation into images of lines from the latter: "A damsel with no human face / lets herself be pushed to shore by Zephyr / floating on a shell; / and heaven seems to rejoice at the sight."

The two embracing figures are Zephyr and Aura, the two winds that blow the shell bearing the charming goddess to shore, while the young woman waiting for her with a flowered piece of cloth is interpreted either as one of the Horae, the nymphs who attend Venus, or as one of the Graces who has been given the task of weaving a mantle to clothe the goddess.

Sandro Botticelli

■ *Madonna del Magnificat*
Room 10/14
panel, diam. 118 cm
Set in its marvelous original frame, the picture constitutes, along with the other celebrated tondo depicting the *Madonna della Melograna*, an illustrious example of private patronage. Its date is still uncertain, with critics assigning it to somewhere between 1481 and 1485. The picture takes its name from the book in which the Madonna is writing, open at the text of the *Magnificat*. This unusual iconography proved highly popular and has often been imitated. While the harmonies of curved lines and the pale but vivid color ensure the beauty typical of Botticelli's painting, the picture is also an example of a studied and skillful fitting together of forms, an allusive interweaving of gazes, and of the use of the circular shape, a recurrent symbol of perfection in the fifteenth century, enhanced by effects resembling those of a distorting mirror.

Hugo van der Goes (Ghent ca. 1440 – Roode Clooster, Brussels, 1482)

■ *The Portinari Altarpiece*
Room 10/14
panel, 253x586 cm
This imposing work has become a symbol of the artistic, commercial, and cultural links that developed between Florence and Flanders over the course of the fifteenth century.
In fact it was commissioned by Tommaso Portinari, an agent of the Medici bank in Bruges. Along with his wife and children, he is portrayed with the precise detail of Flemish art in the side panels. Completed by 1478, the triptych was brought to Florence in 1483 and was placed on the high altar of the church of Sant'Egidio in the Spedale di Santa Maria Nuova, founded by Folco Portinari.
This wonderful compendium of the characteristics of Flemish painting exercised a great and lasting influence over the Florentine art of the late fifteenth century. Painters were struck by the suggestive arrangement of the central scene, organized around an empty space with the Madonna and Child at its center, and by the virtuosity of the still life in the foreground. Above all, however, they were impressed by the

In confirmation of Vasari's account, recent radiographic analyses have identified Leonardo's hand in the delicate face of the angel on the left and the hazy landscape in the background, but it is more and more widely accepted that Lorenzo di Credi and Botticelli were responsible for the other interventions in the painting.

extraordinary realism of the rough and artless faces of the shepherds, depicted with pitiless accuracy. It is plain that Ghirlandaio was thinking about the picture when he painted the same subject for the Sassetti Chapel in the church of Santa Trinita a few years later.

Andrea di Francesco di Cione, called **Verrocchio** (Florence 1435 – Venice 1488) and **Leonardo da Vinci** (Vinci 1452 – Amboise 1519)
■ *Baptism of Christ*
Room 15
panel, 180x152 cm
Together with the picture of a *Madonna and Child* in the Berlin State Museums, this *Baptism* is the only surviving painting by the famous sculptor.
Vasari tells the anecdote of the artist's resolution "never to take up a brush again," after seeing himself outclassed by his young pupil Leonardo, and it must have been in this work that the latter first tried his hand. The same source, in fact, indicates that his pupil was responsible for the left-hand part of the picture, while the two adult figures in a drier and sculptural style were surely the work of Verrocchio.

Leonardo da Vinci

■ *Annunciation*

Room 15

panel, 98x217 cm

Leonardo was still very young and under the
influence of his master Verrocchio when he
painted, in 1472-75, the *Annunciation* for the
church of San Bartolomeo at Monteoliveto, near
Florence. His sculptor teacher seems to have left
his mark on the lavish decoration of the lectern,
whose classical design, together with the still
academic and statuesque treatment of the figures,
has led critics in the past to attribute the work
to Domenico Ghirlandaio. In fact there is no
definitive proof that the work is by Leonardo,
and the attribution rests on stylistic considerations.
The stretch of dark trees, with its features typical
of the Tuscan landscape, from the cypresses to
the flowery meadow and the clipped trees of the
Italian-style garden, constitutes a studied
backdrop, beyond which the horizon fades away
in a very early example of Leonardo's *sfumato*.

in Milan. Men and horses rotate like a vortex around the Holy Family and the astounding event seems to have been used by Leonardo as a pretext for the representation of movement, a central element in his reflections on the world and nature.

Pietro Vannucci, called **Perugino**
(Città della Pieve ca. 1448 – Fontignano 1523)
■ *Madonna and Child with Saints John the Baptist and Sebastian*
Room 15
panel, 178x164 cm
Vasari was greatly impressed by the St. Sebastian in this picture, brought fully back to life by the recent restoration, and the figure is undoubtedly worthy of the writer's praise in the handling of the foreshortened

face and in its elegant nudity, barely concealed by the thin loincloth. The picture, signed and dated (1493) on the scroll set on the base of the throne, was painted for a chapel in the church of San Domenico at Fiesole. It is a typical example of Perugino's clear and terse devotional painting, in which the figures moved by fervent religious feelings are set against a background made up of luminous glimpses of landscape.

Leonardo da Vinci
■ *Adoration of the Magi*
Room 15
panel, 243x246 cm
The haziness of the scene stems in part from the fact that the work was left unfinished when Lorenzo the Magnificent sent Leonardo, in 1482, to the court of Ludovico il Moro, in Milan. The Augustinian monks of San Donato a Scopeto, who had commissioned it from the artist, never saw it completed and were obliged to order a picture of the same subject from Filippino Lippi.
Yet it is amazing to see how this work, painted at such an early stage in the artist's career, displays many of the characteristics of his later production: the original interpretation of the revelation of Christ's divinity that arouses wonder and excitement in the worshippers will be found again, for example, in the apostles of the *Last Supper*

Agnolo Bronzino (Florence 1503 – 1572)
■ *Eleonora of Toledo with her Son Giovanni*
Room 18
panel, 115x96 cm
Duchess Eleonora, daughter of the Spanish viceroy in Naples, is portrayed with her second son Giovanni (1545-46) in one of the most famous pictures by this refined court painter. She is wearing an elegant dress sewn from costly fabrics and decorated with sumptuous Spanish embroidery, but her expression conveys a hint of melancholy that is scarcely concealed by the formality of the portrait. Devoted to her husband and to their numerous children, she was not much loved by their subjects, who may not have approved of her foreign origin.

Agnolo Bronzino
■ *Portraits of Bartolomeo and Lucrezia Panciatichi*
Room 18
panels, 104x84 cm; 102x85 cm
Here we find, set against the backdrop of well-defined works of architecture in the Florentine style, two elegant portraits of Bartolomeo Panciatichi, a wealthy merchant from Pistoia with commercial interests in Lyons and an influential diplomat of the Medicean court, and his wife Lucrezia Pucci. The high rank of the subjects is reflected in the dignity of their clothing, which the painter describes in minute detail, from the fine "cut" sleeves of the man's jacket to the refined jewelry worn by Lucrezia and the inscription in French on her necklace ("Sans fin amour dure"), alluding to marital fidelity and her husband's post on the other side of the Alps.
The figures of the Panciatichi husband and wife, like the neighboring ones of the Medici family, represent the peak of Bronzino's portraiture.

Jacopo Carrucci, called **Pontormo**
(Pontorme, Empoli, 1495 – Florence 1556)
■ *Portrait of Cosimo the Elder*
Room 18
panel, 86x65 cm
Here the *pater patriae* of the Medici family is portrayed posthumously (ca. 1519) in the

manner typical of fifteenth-century portraits on medals. He stands out against the dark ground of the picture, wrapped in a cloak of flaming velvet, with an emaciated physique but a still intense gaze. The bough of laurel, set at his right, is an allegorical allusion to the Medici dynasty's capacity for regeneration – as is the Virgilian motto inscribed on the scroll: UNO AVULSO NON DEFICIT ALTER – which had been interrupted by the violent death of Duke Alessandro but was restored by the birth of Cosimo, the future grand duke, to the other branch of the family.

Agnolo Bronzino
■ *Portrait of Bia de' Medici*
Room 18
panel, 63x48 cm
This portrait of the charming Bia was the first that Bronzino painted of Cosimo's children. It must date from 1542, the year of the death of this natural daughter of Cosimo, who is still portrayed as a young man in the medal that the little girl is wearing around her neck.

Giovan Battista di Jacopo, called **Rosso Fiorentino**
(Florence 1495 – Fontainebleau 1540)
■ *Angel playing a Lute*
Room 18
panel, 39x47 cm
This small panel, probably a fragment of some unknown altarpiece by Rosso (a hypothesis supported by recent reflectographic evidence) that was painted sometime around the 1420s, instills a sense of serenity and affection. Present in the Tribuna ever since 1605, it was long thought to be a work in its own right, perhaps a homage paid by Rosso to Pope Leo X. This old misunderstanding in no way lessens the poetic lyricism of the composition – a sort of graceful diversion in a body of work that often had dramatic tones – which has made it justly famous.

Piero di Cosimo (Florence 1461/2 – 1521)
■ *Liberation of Andromeda*
Room 19
panel, 70x123 cm

This work formed part of a series of pictures representing *Scenes from the Legend of Prometheus*, painted for the salon of Filippo Strozzi's palace by this bizarre and troubled painter, torn between the world of fantasy and a desire to make use of elements of precise realism. In this painting, in fact, it is still possible to make out the scheme of composition typical of the fifteenth century, but immersed in a completely new atmosphere, where the lustrous colors display a liveliness that is already wholly Mannerist, an effect that Piero was able to obtain through his extraordinary technical mastery of the medium of oil painting.

According to the most recent interpretation the picture alludes to the return of the Medici family to power – an event that took place in 1512, the year before the Prometheus cycle was commissioned (1513-15) – after the interlude of the republic, symbolically represented by the tree stump sending out shoots in the middle of the painting. Filippo Strozzi was related to the Medici and this explains the choice of theme and the inclusion in the picture of many portraits of members of the family. The elderly man on the right, looking toward the observer, has been recognized as a self-portrait of the artist.

Albrecht Dürer (Nuremberg 1471 – 1528)
■ *Adoration of the Magi*
Room 20
panel, 99x113 cm

Part of a dismembered polyptych, which critics have hypothesized to be the *Jobach Altarpiece*, it was painted in 1504 for Frederick the Wise. It is one of the great German painter's works that most eloquently testifies to his love of Italian art. In fact there hints of Leonardo's *Adoration* in the group of horsemen in the background, and of Mantegna in the accurate depiction of works of architecture with crumbling arches. At the time Dürer painted it, he had already been to Venice, where he had been greatly impressed by the Venetian use of color. This influence is combined here with careful draftsmanship, perhaps derived from his father's activity as a goldsmith. The painter, who was always inclined to give his own features to the figures in his works, could not fail to include a self-portrait, this time in the guise of the most opulently dressed of the Wise Men.

Giovanni Bellini (Venice 1432/33 – 1516)
■ *Sacred Allegory*
Room 21
panel, 73x119 cm
No convincing interpretation has yet been found for the iconography of this picture. Some have seen it as an unusual version of the *Sacra Conversazione*, the Virgin and Child with saints, others as an allegory of Mercy and Justice, and yet others as an intellectual meditation prompted by the artist's contact with learned Humanistic circles in Venice, perhaps intended for Isabella d'Este's Studiolo in Mantua. One of the hypotheses put forward, in fact, is that it is the figurative translation of a passage from *De vero falsoque bono*, an erudite work by Lorenzo Valla. According to this view, the painting represents infinite Happiness, Christian Serenity. The date assigned to the work varies as much as the interpretations, with some scholars placing it as early as the end of the 1470s while the majority prefer

some time around the end of the fifteenth century. Thus it is a painting as difficult as it is fascinating and unusual. It displays the characteristics of Venetian painting, from the landscape steeped in golden light, an anticipation of Giorgione, to the polychrome Venetian marble.

Lucas Cranach the Elder
(Kronach 1472 – Weimar 1553)
■ *Adam and Eve*
Room 20
panels, 172x63 cm, 167x61 cm
The representation of naked bodies against a dark ground is a theme at which Cranach often tried his hand and one that was common in Northern European painting. This same room in the Uffizi, devoted to German painting, contains another diptych of *Adam and Eve*, by Hans Baldung Grien, which is a copy of the one by Dürer in the Prado. Unlike Dürer, however, Cranach did

not attempt to depict nude bodies according to the ideals of beauty and harmony, but offered a version dominated by the sensually allusive sinuosity of the outlines.

Albrecht Altdorfer

(Regensburg? ca. 1480 – 1538)

■ *Martyrdom of Saint Florian;*
Leave-Taking of Saint Florian

Room 22

panels, 76x67 cm, 81x67 cm

These pictures come from the polyptych painted for the church of St. Florian in Linz (Austria) and now split up among various countries in Europe. They stand out for their bold colors and the emphasis given to the expressions of the figures, set in familiar and clearly recognizable locations of the Austrian countryside. Once again nature plays a predominant role in the artist's painting.

Attributed to **Giorgio Zorzi**, called **Giorgione** (Castelfranco Veneto ca. 1477 – Venice 1510)

■ *Portrait of Captain with Groom*

Room 21

canvas, 90x73 cm

The recent restoration (1990) has given the

reflections on the armor of the burly captain all their original luster. There is some uncertainty over the picture's attribution, though the light that plays over the bodies and fades into the shadows is typical of Giorgionesque circles. It dates from the first decade of the sixteenth century and entered the Uffizi in the nineteenth century.

Hans Memling

(Seligenstadt ca. 1435 – Bruges 1494)

■ *Portrait of an Unknown Man*

Room 22

panel, 38x27 cm

There are a number of precious examples of Flemish portraiture in the Uffizi, and this fine picture that used to be in the Corsini

Collection is one. We do not know the identity of the person portrayed by the artist at a fairly late stage in his career – at least to judge by the luminosity of the landscape in the background, typical of his later production – but he may have been a member of the large Florentine colony in Bruges. But the fact that this portrait has also been attributed to Antonello da Messina is indicative of the close ties that existed between the culture of these two areas in the second half of the fifteenth century.

Andrea Mantegna
(Isola di Carturo 1431 – Mantua 1506)
■ Triptych depicting the *Epiphany, Circumcision, and Ascension*
Room 23
panel, 86x161 cm
The three panels, assembled in an arbitrary manner in the nineteenth century, may have been part of the decoration of a chapel in the Ducal Palace in Mantua, for which they were painted in 1464. They show Mantegna's meticulous draftsmanship as well as his lucid

coloring, a fine example of which can also be seen in the nearby *Portrait of a Man*. The right-hand panel representing the *Circumcision*, in particular, set in a complex architectural structure, demonstrates the painter's refined culture and passion for classical antiquity.

Antonio Allegri, called Correggio
(Correggio 1489 – 1534)
■ *The Virgin adoring the Child*
Room 23
canvas, 81x77 cm
A late work by Correggio (1524-26) that displays a harmonious balance of forms and colors, it is the best-known of the three paintings by the great Emilian artist in the room dedicated to him. It is a wonderful representation of the relationship between mother and son, a theme tackled by the painter several times with excellent results. The impression of a tender and intimate exchange between the two figures is accentuated by the few and simple elements of which the landscape is composed, while the only hint of monumentality is provided by the

majestic classical column in the background. It is a perfect and at the same time profoundly humane composition, in which the atmosphere of Leonardo is combined with the purity of Raphael.

Michelangelo Buonarroti

(Caprese, Arezzo, 1475 – Rome 1564)

■ *Holy Family with the Young Saint John,* known as the *Doni Tondo*

Room 25

panel, diam. 120 cm

This is one of the most important pictures in the museum and the only panel painting unquestionably by the celebrated sculptor and fresco painter. The restoration has revealed its splendid sixteenth-century coloring, still set in the refined original frame. Traditionally it has been regarded as a wedding gift to Agnolo Doni and Maddalena Strozzi (the couple portrayed by Raphael in the famous pictures in the Galleria Palatina), who were married in 1504, though recently it has been suggested that it was linked with the birth

of their eldest daughter and the date shifted to 1506-8).

His representation of the Holy Family revolutionizes the traditional composition, establishing a balance of forces that pivots on the bust of the sinewy figure of the Virgin, as she twists around to take the Child. In this virtuoso exercise in *ponderatio* (balancing of weights) for which Michelangelo is so famed in his sculpture, we seem to find a perfect application of his celebrated declaration that painting approaches perfection "the more it goes toward the relief." The representation of the figures, in fact, moves beyond naturalism

and anticipates motifs and solutions typical of Mannerism. Michelangelo's picture can be said to serve as a splendid introduction to this artistic current, well documented in the following rooms of the gallery. This extraordinary effect – so close to that of the frescoes in the Sistine Chapel – is enhanced by the use Michelangelo makes of color, laid on in such a way that no trace of brushwork can be discerned and based on shimmering tones that seem to be intended to convey the ever-changing nature of reality. The figures in the background are a testimony to the artist's study of classical antiquity. Precise references have been detected to certain Hellenistic sculptures, from the *Belvedere Apollo* to the *Laocoön*, the famous sculpture discovered in 1506, and it is this that has suggested the later date assigned to the work.

Mariotto Albertinelli

(Florence 1474 – 1515)

■ *Visitation*

Room 25

panel, 232.5x146.5 cm

The date of the work is inscribed on the pillars decorated with grotesques: 1503. It comes from the Florentine church of San Michele in Palchetto, suppressed at the end of the eighteenth century. It is generally held to be the work of Albertinelli, though a major contribution by Fra Bartolomeo has been suspected in the past, perhaps on the grounds of Vasari's dismissal of Mariotto as a minor figure, an assistant to the friar with whom, moreover, he painted pictures in collaboration. In reality, however, an intervention by Fra Bartolomeo, who had given up painting in those very years to enter the Dominican order, is only feasible at the planning stage.

So Albertinelli is fully responsible for the vivid and shimmering colors brought to light by the recent restoration, which can be considered a worthy antecedent to the later developments in Florentine Mannerist painting. This bold use of color, on the other hand, is combined with a severe handling of the architecture and figures that derives from the tradition of Perugino.

Raffaello Sanzio, called Raphael

(Urbino 1483 – Rome 1520)

■ *Leo X with Cardinals Giulio de' Medici and Luigi de' Rossi*

Room 26

panel, 155.5x119.5 cm

Along with the nearby *Madonna of the Goldfinch*, this is the most famous of Raphael's works on show in the gallery.

It is a late work by the artist (1517-18), which has always been greatly esteemed by the critics. Vasari admired it for its perfect rendering of the pile of the velvet, the relief of the figures, and at the same time the attention paid to details like the chased silver bell – exemplifying the refined tastes of the powerful pope and discerning patron of the arts – and the realistic depiction of the gold knob on the chair: with the meticulousness that we might have expected from a Flemish painter, "like a mirror" this "reflects the light from the windows, the Pope's shoulders, and the walls around the room." All these characteristics are now clearly visible after the picture's restoration.

It has recently been observed that the figures of the two cardinals may have been added at a later date, since radiographic examinations do not reveal the same tracings as are apparent underneath the figure of the pope. In fact the features of Luigi de' Rossi, on Leo X' left, have the harder lines more typical of his pupil Giulio Romano's style, while recent critics have suggested that the other figure, with its very solid composition, is the work of Sebastiano del Piombo.

Andrea del Sarto (Florence 1486 – 1530)
■ *Madonna delle Arpie*
Room 26
panel, 207x178 cm

This picture entered the Uffizi as a result of the insistence of Grand Prince Ferdinando de' Medici. In order to get hold of the work, which he had fallen in love with, he undertook to restore the church of the Florentine monastery of San Francesco de' Macci, for which it had been painted almost two centuries earlier, and provide a copy to put in its place. Its curious name (*Madonna of the Harpies*) derives from the monstrous figures on the base that supports the sacred group, though these are more likely to represent the locusts mentioned by St. John in *Revelation*, the text on which the altarpiece's iconography is based.

As in the majority of his works, Andrea uses a

concise and symmetrical composition typical of Fra Bartolomeo's style, but handles the paint in a freer manner, combining great vitality with soft brushwork and achieving that "flawless" result so admired by Vasari.

Pontormo
■ *Supper at Emmaus*
Room 27
canvas, 230x173 cm

The picture was painted (in 1525) for the guest quarters of the charterhouse of Galluzzo, along with the famous cycle of frescoes depicting *Scenes of the Passion*, still in its original location. The work immediately met with the approval of his contemporaries and prompted an enthusiastic response from Vasari, but the judgments of critics have been more than flattering right up to the present day. In particular, attention has always been drawn to the realistic depiction of the figures, with the friars' faces portraying people who had actually lived, and to the foretaste of the seventeenth-century realism of Caravaggio and Velázquez that can be discerned in the incomparable still life set out on the table. But the whole composition is steeped in a mystical atmosphere and the various figures participate in this climate of intense spirituality with the sense of disquiet that is aroused by events of a supernatural character.

Tiziano Vecellio, called **Titian**
(Pieve di Cadore ca. 1488 – Venice 1576)
■ *Venus of Urbino*
Room 28
canvas, 119x165 cm
The work, painted in 1538 or slightly earlier,
takes its name from its client, Guidobaldo
della Rovere. It is one of the artist's most
famous pictures, and holds a prominent place
among the many female figures that emerged
from his brush, all linked together by the
thread of sensuality and *joie de vivre*. There are
still differing interpretations of the significance
of the composition, but there is no doubt over
its nature as an allegorical representation,
perhaps an allusion to conjugal love as
suggested by the bouquet of roses in Venus's
hand – a symbol of constancy in love – and
the pot of myrtle, another symbol of love, on
the windowsill.

Francesco Mazzola, called **Parmigianino**
(Parma 1504 – Casalmaggiore 1540)
■ *Madonna and Child with Angels* or
Madonna with the Long Neck
Room 29
panel, 219x135 cm

Today this work is considered one of the masterpieces of Emilian Mannerism, but in the past it provoked varying reactions from the critics and may not have been greatly valued even by the artist himself, who left it unfinished. Perhaps they were disturbed by the impression of affectation that appeared to derive from the verticality of the composition as a whole – overlaid by the profile of the large, sleeping Child – and the grace of the group of angels, which look as if they have been inserted like cameos. In truth this work was to leave its mark on much of the Emilian art of the seventeenth century and even on certain much later tendencies of eighteenth- and nineteenth-century neoclassicism.

Giovan Battista Luteri, called **Dosso Dossi** (Ferrara ca. 1489 – 1542)
■ *Witchcraft* or *Allegory of Hercules*
Room 31
canvas, 143x144 cm
While the attribution to Dosso is virtually undisputed, there are doubts over the subject depicted by this eccentric Emilian artist, court painter to Duke Ercole II. It might be a representation of Hercules under the influence of Queen Omphale, but it is more likely an allusion to the casting of magic spells intended to make the young man in the center holding a rock fall in love with the woman seated near him. The colors are the vivid and brilliant ones typical of Dossi's style and the resemblance of the faces to caricatures is a mark of the Ferrarese school.

Sebastiano Luciani, called **Sebastiano del Piombo** (Venice ca. 1485 – Rome 1547)
■ *Death of Adonis*
Room 32
canvas, 189x285 cm
The two works by Sebastiano in the Uffizi, this well-known picture (one of the most important to have been damaged by the bomb in 1993) and the *Portrait of a Woman*, reveal how the artist was able to blend the influence of the Venetian culture of Giorgione with the Roman one of Michelangelo, from which the sculptural anatomical forms are derived. When Sebastiano came to Rome at the invitation of Agostino Chigi, the wealthy banker of Pope Julius II who wanted him to decorate his villa on the Tiber (now the Farnesina), Michelangelo was busy painting the ceiling of the Sistine Chapel and Raphael the Stanze in the Vatican. The first work that Sebastiano painted in Rome was this *Adonis*, which marked a fundamental turning point in his production and a symbol of the encounter between the monumental classicism of Roman form and the coloring of Venetian art, with the landscape and human figure depicted in a blend of colors that was admired by everyone. The subject is based on a text by Francesco Colonna, who was well-known to Venetian artists, and illustrates the tragic moment when Adonis is killed by a wild boar, but the picture is filled with complicated allegorical meanings that enrich its interpretation.
The celebrated view of Venice in the background may have been the artist's tribute to the city that he had recently left.

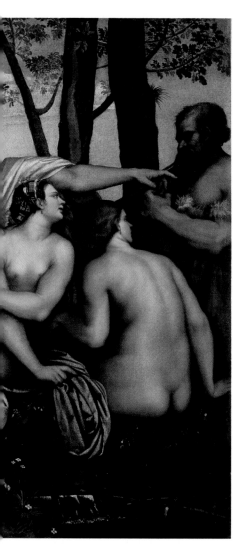

Paolo Caliari, called **Veronese**
(Verona 1528 – Venice 1588)
■ *Martyrdom of Saint Justine*
Room 34
canvas, 103x113 cm
The painting was acquired by Cardinal
Leopoldo de' Medici in 1675. According to an
old source it was painted around 1550, but
experts have dated it to about twenty years
later (ca. 1573) on the basis of stylistic
considerations. The restoration has brought to
light particularly bright colors typical of
Venetian painting, while the customary works
of architecture that provide the setting for
many works by Venetian artists of the time are
relegated to the background, accentuating the
monumental appearance of the figures placed
at stage front.

Lorenzo Lotto
(Venice ca. 1480 – Loreto ca. 1556)
■ *The Chastity of Susanna*
Room 32
panel, 66x50 cm
The picture comes from the Florentine
Contini-Bonacossi collection and was
acquired by the gallery in 1975. It is a work
that sums up the various influences on the
artist's style, filled with references to Lombard
and Venetian culture as is immediately
apparent from the tranquil landscape of
Giorgionesque derivation. The elevated point
of view allows the eye to move beyond the
agitation of the scene in the foreground and
gaze into the distance, a scheme that he was to
use again in the celebrated and later
Annunciation in Recanati. The work is dated
(1517) and signed at the bottom, on the side
of the basin.

Jacopo Robusti, called **Tintoretto**
(Venice 1518 – 1594)

■ *Leda and the Swan*
Room 34
canvases, 146x148 cm; 167x221 cm
It is a curious fact that the Uffizi has ended up with two pictures of the same subject by Tintoretto, but painted at different times and coming from different sources. The restoration of both pictures has confirmed their authorship and the earlier date assigned to the *Leda* from the collection of Rodolfo Siviero, while revealing the undisputed quality of Tintoretto's brushwork in the other painting, which entered the gallery in the nineteenth century with a generic attribution to the painter's workshop: the silky vibration of the light, the softness of the flesh tones, and the way that the foreshortened figures almost slide past one another are all unmistakable marks of the master's touch.

Federico Barocci (Urbino 1535 – 1612)
■ *Madonna del Popolo*
Room 35
panel, 359x252 cm
The recent restoration has confirmed the status of this picture by Barocci – one of the leading painters in Europe in the seventeenth century – as a masterpiece. It was finished in 1579 after several years work and a whole series of preparatory sketches, and put on show in the parish church of Arezzo, where it immediately proved a great success. Many Tuscan artists influenced by the Counter Reformation made a pilgrimage to Arezzo to draw inspiration from the work: among the best-known, Cigoli, Pagani, Empoli, and Passignano.
The painting is still striking today for its wonderful, delicately shaded colors and its scene thronged with figures. The sacred story is narrated in a domestic and familiar

key (the artist places the Redeemer himself close to the crowd of ordinary people) and it is possible to make out a rich range of contemporary physiognomies.

Pieter Paul Rubens (Siegen, Westphalia, 1577 – Antwerp 1640)
■ *Judith and Holofernes*
Room 41
canvas, 113x89 cm
The cleaning carried out in order to repair the damage inflicted by the recent bomb attack (1993) has made it possible to assign the work to Rubens with confidence, following elimination of the repainting to which it had been subjected. Judith's face, in particular, has regained the soft luminosity and opulence typical of Rubens, and the influence of two paintings of the same subject by Veronese can now be detected.
Curiously, a number of nineteenth-century additions have disappeared, such as the golden fringes of the drape and the pearl necklace around Judith's neck which masked a poorly executed retouch, and in general the picture has acquired a new freshness and delicacy of the features.

Diego Rodríguez de Silva y Velázquez (Seville 1599 – Madrid 1660) and workshop
■ *Equestrian Portrait of Philip IV of Spain*
Room 41
canvas, 338x267 cm
The painting, which was long attributed to the school of Rubens, in fact turns out to be a copy of the original by that painter which was destroyed by the fire at the Alcázar in 1734. However it does present a number of variations with respect to the original portrait, even in the features of the king. Rubens had painted Philip at the age of twenty-two, wearing a hat with white plumes. Fifteen years later, Velázquez's version shows the king at an older age and now wearing the hat with red plumes that appears in several of the pictures painted in those years. After the restoration carried out to repair the damage inflicted in 1993, all the vitality of the Spanish artist's style has been revealed, and is apparent in the head of the powerful horse as well as the figure of the sovereign. As far as the landscape and the allegorical figures are concerned, however, the resemblance to the earlier Flemish painting is stronger and they are more likely to have been the work of assistants.

youth. Quite apart from these attempts at historical identification, however, what is really striking about this painting is the extraordinary physicality of the figure taken from real life and used to represent the pagan god. A realism that the young artist, only just over twenty at the time the picture was painted (1595-96), must have derived from the culture of his native Lombardy.

Caravaggio
■ *Sacrifice of Isaac*
Room 43
canvas, 104x135 cm
This picture from a more mature period than the *Bacchus* (ca. 1603) was donated to the Uffizi by an English Pre-Raphaelite painter who used to live in Tuscany, John Fairfax Murray (1917).
Just like in the *Bacchus*, however, the way that this episode from the Bible is handled offers us a fine example of the realistic vein that runs through the whole of the artist's work. The beautiful landscape in the Venetian manner, relegated to the background, shows that Caravaggio's overriding interest lay in the human figure. The figure of Isaac has often been identified as "Giulietto," the model and assistant of his early paintings.

Michelangelo Merisi, called **Caravaggio**
(Caravaggio or Milan 1570/71 – Porto Ercole 1610)
■ *Bacchus*
Room 43
canvas, 95x85 cm
This representation of Bacchus, the ancient god of wine and drunkenness, in the dress of a contemporary young man and in an almost sacrilegious pose, is an early example of Caravaggio's new and unusual approach to art, in which the classical myths are reinterpreted in terms of a faithful observation of reality. There has been much discussion in the past over the identity of the young Bacchus, often considered a self-portrait of the artist but more recently thought to be a little-known Sicilian painter who lived with Caravaggio in his

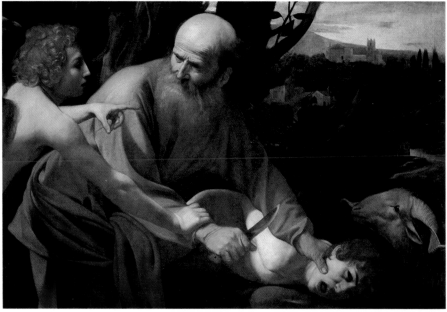

Annibale Carracci

(Bologna 1560 – Rome 1609)

■ *Venus, Satyr, and Cupids*

Room 43

canvas, 112x142 cm

This beautiful early picture by Carracci
(ca. 1588) already displays the principal
characteristics of the work he produced later
in his career in the decoration of noble palaces
in Rome. The sensual figure of the goddess,
caressed by a golden and harmonious light and
inspired by the local Mannerist tradition, shows
the direct influence of the great Venetian
painting of Titian and Tintoretto, but given
here a sharper, naturalistic immediacy.

Claude Gellée, called **Claude Lorrain**

(Chamagne, Nancy, 1600 – Rome 1682)

■ *Harbor with Medici Villa*

Room 43

canvas, 102x133 cm

This picture was painted by the famous French landscapist for Cardinal Carlo de' Medici, who frequented the circle of Christina of Sweden in Rome, where the painter worked. He was celebrated for his ability to devise fantastic landscapes and assemble imaginary scenes out of realistic elements such as the Roman residence of the Medici, which appears here in the background, but facing onto a nonexistent harbor lit up by a magnificent sunset.
The picture is dated 1637.

Rembrandt Harmenszoon van Rijn
(Leiden 1606 – Amsterdam 1669)
■ *Self-portrait as an Old Man*
Room 44
canvas, 74x55 cm
Rembrandt painted a large number of self-portraits. The Uffizi only possesses two of them, one as a young man and this picture, which was also the first of his works to be acquired by the museum. It was probably Grand Duke Cosimo III, who bought the picture directly from the artist's workshop, showing that his fame had spread as far as Italy. But it may also have been a commission

from Cardinal Leopoldo de' Medici, an enthusiastic collector of self-portraits, that brought it to Florence. A work of great quality, it portrays the artist at the age of sixty, dressed in magnificent clothes, a gold chain round his neck, and one of his typical hats.

Jean-Baptiste-Siméon Chardin
(Paris 1699 – 1779)
■ *Girl with Shuttlecock; Boy with House of Cards*
Room 45
canvases, 82x66 cm (each)

Taking his inspiration from the interiors and depictions of simple and serene domestic activities typical of Flemish painting, Chardin became the eighteenth-century poet of genre painting. This pair of children playing with cards and a shuttlecock date from around 1740 and were acquired by the Uffizi in 1951. The figures and objects are set in space with a compositional rigor worthy of Vermeer. Chardin's depiction of the life of the middle classes never gave way to sentimentalism. Rather it was a clear-sighted and probing investigation that derived from the culture of the Enlightenment.

Giuseppe Maria Crespi

(Bologna 1665 – 1747)
■ *The Flea*
Room 45
copper, 46x34 cm
The artist – who spent a happy period in Florence under the patronage of Grand Prince Ferdinando de' Medici – painted not only large pictures of mythological subjects and landscapes, but also delicious genre scenes like this *Flea*, prompted by his encounter with the many Flemish and Dutch paintings in the Medici collections. In any case, these ideas fell on fertile ground as far as the Emilian painter was concerned, with his background in the realism of the school of the Carracci and Guercino.

Francisco de Goya y Lucientes

(Fuendetodos, Saragossa, 1746 – Bordeaux 1828)
■ *Portrait of Countess de Chinchón Standing*
Room 45
canvas, 220x140 cm
Here Goya portrays the daughter of Don Luis of Bourbon, and therefore the niece of Philip V of Spain. The artist knew his subject and was therefore able to convey, with frank psychological penetration, the sadness of a woman trapped in an unhappy marriage with the minister Manuel de Godoy.

The noblewoman is fashionably attired in a high-cut dress that Empress Josephine was later to make famous all over Europe, though with a more severe line that eliminated the filmy Spanish gauze so skillfully depicted in this portrait. The work dates from Goya's maturity (1799-1801), when he was principal painter to the court of Spain.

PALAZZO
VECCHIO

More than any other building in Florence, the massive walls of Palazzo Vecchio encapsulate the city's history. In fact the story of the palace, restructured several times over the centuries, mirrors that of the people of Florence and its government. At the time the decision was taken to build it, in 1294, the city was just emerging from a troubled period, in which it had been torn apart by ferocious strife between Guelphs and Ghibellines. The defeat of the latter had coincided with the rise of new social classes, organized into guilds, and the government of the city was placed in the hands of the Gonfalonier of Justice and six Priors, all drawn from the guilds. The latter held office for a period of two months, during which they lived a communal life. The new palace was intended to give the Priors a secure and permanent abode and to be a symbol of their authority. So in 1299 work commenced on the building, which incorporated the remains of the houses of the Ghibelline Uberti family. Vasari attributes its design and construction to Arnolfo di Cambio, claiming that he took his inspiration from the castle his father had built for the Counts Guidi at Poppi. By 1302 the exterior of the building had more or less attained the

architect. In 1472, under Lorenzo the Magnificent, work commenced on the major alterations to the Sala Grande on the third floor, completed by Benedetto and Giuliano da Maiano. Later on, further decorations were carried out by painters and sculptors like Domenico Ghirlandaio, Filippino Lippi, and Donatello.

On the death of Lorenzo the Magnificent in 1492 and the subsequent expulsion of the Medici family, the building was taken over by the new republican government, inspired by the fiery preaching of Girolamo Savonarola. The city council was expanded to a total of 1500 members, split into groups of 500, and this made a new Sala del Consiglio, or Council Chamber, essential. Work began on its construction over what is now the Cortile della Doga-

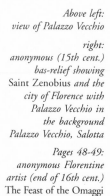

appearance it has today, but with the addition of the rear facade, which has now been covered up by subsequent extensions. A square fortress with rusticated walls, portals, and two rows of mullioned windows with two lights. A gallery runs along all four sides of the building and is decorated with painted coats of arms. The tower is offset from the middle of the palace, as it is built on the foundations of the preexisting Ghibelline tower of the Foraboschi. If we exclude a few fortifications constructed in 1343, during the brief rule of

Gualtieri di Brienne, the first major alterations to the palace were made in the fifteenth century. The triumphant return of Cosimo de' Medici from exile in 1434 and the reestablishment of his authority was followed by the creation of the office of the "Operai di Palazzo" (Palace Trustees), whose job it was to oversee the work of restoring and modernizing the building, a task in which the most important Florentine artists of the fifteenth century were involved. In 1453 the courtyard was restructured by Michelozzo, Cosimo's na in 1495. In 1503 the Gonfalonier of Justice Pier Soderini (Savonarola and his followers had been burned as heretics five years earlier) called on Leonardo da Vinci and Michelangelo to fresco two walls of the Salone dei Cinquecento with scenes of battles won by the Florentine Republic: the former was commissioned to paint the battle of Anghiari and the latter the battle of Cascina. Unfortunately both works met with a similar, unhappy fate: the first began to deteriorate as soon as Leonardo had finished it and was destroyed or covered by later frescoes; the second was never painted because Michelangelo, after drawing the cartoon, which was also destroyed later on, left Florence for Rome.

In 1540 Cosimo I de' Medici, who had come to power with the title of duke, chose the palace as the residence for himself, his wife Eleonora of Toledo, and the court. The work required to adapt the austere building to the needs and tastes of a princely court lasted for over thirty years and the new Quartiere di Leone X and Quartiere degli Elementi were added onto

the east side of the medieval structure. Giorgio Vasari, faithful servant of the Medici family until his death in 1574, was the skillful "director" of this grandiose enterprise and he and his collaborators

were responsible for the decoration of all the interiors, which had remained almost unaltered up until that time. In 1588 Grand Duke Ferdinando, Cosimo's younger son, commissioned new alterations from Bartolomeo Ammannati and Bernardo Buontalenti, who built the facades on Via dei Gondi and Via dei Leoni. In the meantime, however, the grand ducal family had moved to Palazzo Pitti, and Palazzo Vecchio entered a period of slow decline. This did not come to an end until the nineteenth century, when Florence served as the capital of the new kingdom of Italy from 1865 to 1871 and the palace was used as the seat of Parliament. At present the building houses the offices of the mayor, the council, and the municipality of Florence.

Left:
Giuseppe Gherardi
The Feast of the
Omaggi
Florence, Galleria
d'Arte Moderna

Right:
Giovanni Stradano
Fireworks on the
Feast of St John
the Baptist
Palazzo Vecchio

Above:
Andrea Orcagna (attr.)
The Expulsion of the
Duke of Athens
Palazzo Vecchio,
Salotta

Ground Floor

The Cortile di Michelozzo

Surrounded by a portico resting on columns and octagonal pillars, the courtyard was restructured in the Renaissance style by Michelozzo, who also created the two rows of two-light windows and "eyes" on the entresol, once decorated with gold lilies. In 1565, on the occasion of the marriage of Cosimo I's eldest son to Joan of Austria, Giorgio Vasari designed and realized, with the aid of his collaborators, a new decoration, the one we still see today. The columns were covered with gilded stuccowork, the ceilings painted with grotesques, and the walls frescoed with views of the principal cities ruled by the house of Austria. Francesco del Tadda's fountain was set up at the center of the courtyard and topped by Andrea del Verrocchio's *Putto with Dolphin*, brought from the Medici villa of Careggi (the original bronze is now kept inside the palace).

The Cortile di Michelozzo

Center:
the Sala dei Dugento

Left:
Andrea del Verrocchio
Putto with Dolphin
Palazzo Vecchio

Second Floor

The Sala dei Dugento

Part of the fourteenth-century nucleus of the palace, the Room of the Two Hundred used to house the assemblies of the Council of the People, which had two hundred members. In the fifteenth century it was restructured by Benedetto and Giuliano da Maiano, who also installed the coffered ceiling and the friezes with their rich carvings of rosettes, garlands, fleurs-de-lis, and the emblems of the people of Florence. In 1545 Cosimo I commissioned a series of twenty tapestries depicting *Scenes from the Life of the Patriarch Joseph* to hang on the walls. The choice of subject for the cycle, woven to cartoons by Pontormo, Bronzino, and Salviati, left no doubts about the intentions of the duke, who was presenting himself as the guide and savior of his people.

The Salone dei Cinquecento

Designed and built between 1495 and 1496 by Simone del Pollaiolo called Cronaca, this room, intended to house the meetings of the Council of the Florentine Republic and for that reason known as the Hall of the Five Hundred, preserves little of its original appearance today. Cosimo I decided to transform it completely, turning it into a sumptuous setting for official receptions that would celebrate his power and glory. In 1540 Baccio Bandinelli and Giuliano di Baccio

The ceiling of the Salone dei Cinquecento, central section

Above right:
Giorgio Vasari and collaborators
Cosimo I studies Plans for the Capture of Siena
Ceiling of the Salone dei Cinquecento

d'Agnolo were entrusted with the task of realizing this eulogistic program. They built a raised platform on the north side of the Audience Chamber in which sculpture and architecture combined to exalt the figure of Cosimo. The work of transforming the hall was continued by Giorgio Vasari between 1563 and 1565: he raised the height of the room and, with the help of a large group of artists, painted the panels on the ceiling that celebrate the history of Florence and the exploits of Cosimo I, who is depicted in apotheosis in the central tondo, surrounded by the Arts and crowned, like a second Augustus, as the founder of the duchy. Cosimo's military talents are lauded once again in the decoration of the walls (1567-71): the frescoes on the east wall representing the victory over Siena, achieved by the Medici in the space of just thirteen months, face the ones on the west wall depicting the conquest of Pisa, which cost the republic of Florence thirteen long years of warfare. In 1565 a masterpiece by Michelangelo was placed in the hall: *The Spirit of Victory*. The sculptural group, carved for the tomb of Julius II, was given to Cosimo I by the artist's nephew and set up here as an allegory of the victory over Siena and a companion piece to Giambologna's *Florence Victorious over Pisa* (the original of this sculpture is now in the Bargello).

The Salone dei Cinquecento

Below:
Michelangelo
The Spirit of Victory
Salone dei Cinquecento

Francesco I's "Studiolo"

In 1564 Cosimo I's son Francesco took over the reins of government from his father, who retired to live in the Villa di Castello. A man with a melancholic character but penetrating mind, the young duke was a lover of philosophical, alchemical, and scientific studies and would have preferred to stay in the country and devote himself to his reflections and experiments, but was now obliged to install himself in what had been his father's apartments. A collector of minerals, gems, and rare and precious objects, Francesco I needed a "sanctum" in the palace where he could store them and devote himself to his studies in peace and quiet. In 1570 he ordered Vasari to create this study with the help of his entourage of artists. The extremely complex iconographic program was entrusted to the court scholar, Vincenzo Borghini. He came up with a scheme centered on the relationship

Francesco I's Studiolo

Page 56 top:
Giorgio Vasari
The Capture of Pisa
Salone dei Cinquecento

Page 56 bottom:
Giorgio Vasari
The Battle of Marciano
in the Chiana Valley
Salone dei Cinquecento

between Nature and Art (where by art is meant the human manipulation of natural elements) that connected the paintings on the ceiling, the statues in the niches, and the painted panels inserted in the doors of the cabinets with the objects that they contained. Prometheus is depicted at the center of the ceiling, with the symbols of the four elements of nature, Water, Air, Earth, and Fire, at the sides. The subjects painted on the walls also refer to the natural elements and their derivatives through the representation of activities connected with them, the workshops of goldsmiths, glassmakers, and alchemists, and related mythological themes. Owing to the complexity of the conception and the quality of the works produced by artists like Alessandro Allori, Santi di Tito, and Giambologna, the Studiolo is one of the finest examples of Mannerist figurative culture.

Left:
Giovanni Stradano
The Alchemist's
Laboratory
Francesco I's Studiolo

Top right:
Maso da San Friano
The Diamond Mine
Francesco I's Studiolo

below:
Alessandro Fei
The Goldsmith's
Workshop
Francesco I's Studiolo

Page 59 top:
the Sala di Leone X

bottom:
the ceiling of the Sala di
Cosimo il Vecchio

The Quartiere di Leone X

Situated on the second floor, adjacent to the Salone dei Cinquecento, the Apartments of Leo X take their name from the room onto which almost all of its rooms face. In fact each of the rooms is dedicated to a member of the house of Medici, with representations of the salient moments in his life. The choice of episodes is intended to present a picture of exceptional personalities, seen almost as terrestrial gods. The suite of rooms, created in the sixteenth century as a place to hold receptions, was decorated at the same time as the one above it, dedicated to mythological deities. In fact the two apartments were linked by a single iconographic program glorifying Cosimo I and the Medici dynasty, drawn up by the scholar Cosimo Bartoli and executed by Giorgio Vasari and his assistants.

The magnificence of the settings, on which work commenced in 1555, was augmented by gilded stuccos and floors of red and white terra-cotta tiles in patterns that echoed those of the ceilings. On the decoration of the first two rooms, dedicated to Cosimo the Elder and Lorenzo the Magnificent, Vasari's collaborator was Marco da Faenza, a painter with a gift for ornament and a true master of grotesques. In the rooms of Cosimo I, Giovanni dalle Bande Nere, Leo X, and Clement VII, Vasari drew chiefly on the assistance of Stradano, an excellent landscapist who proved to be particularly capable of representing the compositions conceived by Vasari in a fresh and lively style.

The ceiling of the Sala di Giovanni dalle Bande Nere

Giorgio Vasari and Giovanni Stradano The Siege of Florence Sala di Clemente VII

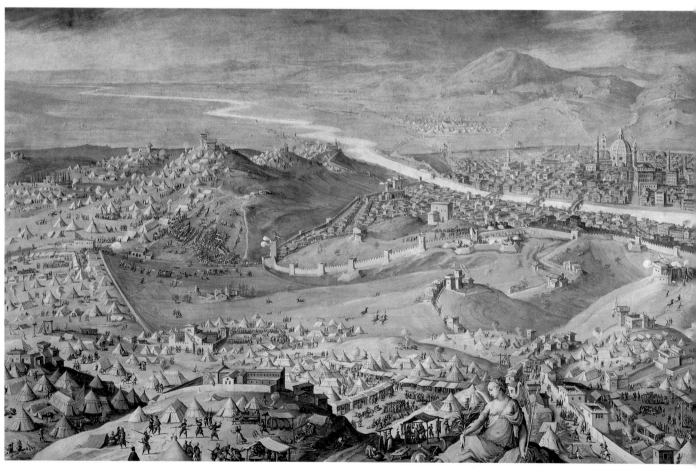

Third Floor

The Quartiere degli Elementi

In the rooms dedicated to the genealogy of the heavenly gods, known as the Apartments of the Elements and decorated by Vasari and his collaborators, the eulogistic intent is plain: a legitimization of Cosimo I's authority. Each room is related to the one underneath in the Apartments of Leo X, creating illustrious allegorical couplings: Cosimo the Elder and Ceres, the goddess of the fertility of nature; Lorenzo the Magnificent and Ops, the goddess of abundance; Cosimo I and Jupiter, the ruler of Olympus; Giovanni dalle Bande Nere and Hercules, the god of indomitable strength, celebrated by his twelve labors; Clement VII and Saturn, the god of time and father of Jupiter; Leo X and the Natural Elements. In this last room the four elements are represented in large images filled with references to Cosimo I.

Other richly decorated rooms are the small Scrittoio di Calliope which Cosimo I used to keep his own rare and precious objects, and the large Terrazzo di Giunone, one of Eleonora di Toledo's favorite places.

The Quartiere di Eleonora

When Cosimo I moved into the palace, he chose the rooms on the second floor for himself, those on the mezzanine for his mother, Maria Salviati, and the ones on the

The Camera Verde,
decorated by Ridolfo
del Ghirlandaio

Above:
the Sala degli Elementi

third floor, once reserved for the collegial life of the Priors, for his wife, Eleonora of Toledo. Battista del Tasso, an architect who had already worked on the palace, was given the task of adapting the old apartments to the needs of the duchess and her household. The first rooms to be decorated were the duchess's private chapel, frescoed by Agnolo Bronzino, the Camera Verde, probably a work room, painted by Ridolfo del Ghirlandaio, and the Scrittoio decorated with grotesques by Francesco Salviati. In the chapel Bronzino, an elegant and refined artist, depicted four scenes taken from the Old Testament in almost profane tones. The walls are thronged with a multitude of figures that are either nude or richly draped in clothing of shimmering and brilliant colors, fully revived by a recent restoration. The other rooms, renovated at a later stage by Vasari, were intended for Eleonora's ladies-in-waiting. Each was dedicated to the virtues of illustrious women of antiquity (the Sabines, Esther, Penelope, and Gualdrada). Unfortunately the apartments were never used by the duchess, who died of malaria at Pisa in 1562.

The Cappella dei Priori

Built in 1511 by Baccio d'Agnolo as a replacement for an earlier chapel whose exact location is not known, the Chapel of the Priors was decorated in 1514 by Ridolfo del Ghirlandaio. The painter created a complex symbolic cycle composed of sacred figures and classical motifs, columns, capitals, and gilded cornices with quotations from the Old and New Testament alluding to the righteous exercise of justice, a clear admonishment to the Priors who used to gather here in prayer before going into the rooms of the Council.

The Sala dell'Udienza

This room, created in 1472 by the subdivision of the Sala Grande, located above the Sala dei Dugento on the second floor, was intended for use as an Audience Chamber by the Seigniory. The dividing wall was built by Benedetto da Maiano, who also collaborated with his brother Giuliano on the marble doorway with the statue of *Justice* on top. Giuliano made the inlaid leaves of the door and the wonderful coffered ceiling, with its superb carving and gilding. In 1543, as part of the major renovation commissioned by Cosimo I to adapt the palace to its new role as a ducal residence, Francesco Salviati was given the task of painting the room with a complex cycle of frescoes based on the life of Marcus Furius Camillus, the general who saved republican Rome from invasion by the Gauls, in a clear allusion to the virtues of the new ruler of Florence. Under the brush of Salviati, Florentine by birth but "Roman" by training, the walls took on the appearance of great, colored "bas-reliefs," in which scenes of battles and triumphs alternate with allegorical figures, festoons, and trophies, with direct references to the ancient world.

The Sala dei Gigli

Created, like the previous one, by the partitioning of the fourteenth-century Sala Grande, the Room of Lilies gets its name from the decoration of the walls and ceiling. It is the only room that still has the appearance it was given in the fifteenth century. In fact the fine marble doorway with a statue of the *Baptist*, the work of Benedetto da Maiano, dates from the 1470s and the rich carvings of the frieze and ceiling were made, like the ones in the Sala dell'Udienza, by Giuliano da Maiano and his collaborators. Domenico Ghirlandaio's monumental fresco on the east wall, depicting *Saint Zenobius Enthroned*, was painted just a decade later. The figure of the bishop, patron saint of Florence, along with those of the martyrs Stephen and Lawrence and eminent

personages of ancient Rome, testified to the religious sentiments and social commitment on which the political ideals of the Florentine Republic were founded. Since 1988 the room has also housed one of Donatello's masterpieces, *Judith and Holofernes*. Cast around 1457 for Cosimo the

Elder, the bronze group representing the Jewish heroine in the act of beheading the Assyrian general Holofernes, after seducing him and getting him drunk, had been placed in front of the Palazzo della Signoria after the expulsion of the Medici, as a symbol of victory over tyranny.

The Sala dei Gigli

Above:
the Sala dell'Udienza

Page 62, left:
Eleonora of Toledo's Chapel frescoed by Bronzino

right:
the Cappella dei Priori

Museo del
Bargello

Among the many towers that soar above the roofs of Florence, not far off and just a little lower than the majestic one of Palazzo Vecchio, rises the battlemented tower of the Bargello. Its solidity, obvious in comparison with the slender Gothic campanile of the nearby church of Badia, is reminiscent of castles and fortifications. It is in fact one of the oldest buildings in the city (predating even Palazzo Vecchio), erected in the middle of the thirteenth century, during the period when Florence was a commune, to house the highest representative of the Florentine Commune known as the Capitano del Popolo. According to Vasari, the original nucleus of the building, the part facing onto via del Proconsolo, is the work of Lapo Tedesco, father of the celebrated architect of Florence Cathedral, Arnolfo di Cambio, but it is more likely that it was built by the Dominicans Fra Sisto and Fra Ristoro, the architects of the church of Santa Maria Novella.

Subsequently the building was extended along via Ghibellina, the street that was opened up, as its name suggests, during the period of Ghibelline rule to permit rapid exodus from the city in case of need, as well as to provide the imperial army with easy access to the heart of Florence.

It was then enclosed by a courtyard that was embellished with merlons, mullioned windows with two lights, and Gothic decorations, later completed by the staircase with the beautiful loggia ("verone"). In the meantime the seat of the Capitano del Popolo became, with the return of the Guelphs, the seat of the Podestà and later the place where justice was administered, acquiring a more and more pivotal role in city life. The bell on the ancient tower of the "Volognona," rebuilt after the fire that raged through the whole building in 1304, told the citizenry when condemned criminals were receiving the last sacraments. The wrought-iron work on the outside walls, still visible today, was used to display the enemies of the commune in effigy, both as a warning and so that they could receive further abuse, while a

box set under the loggia of the courtyard was used to receive anonymous denunciations of citizens and nobles.

Following the restorations carried out in the nineteenth century, the courtyard and some of the rooms are now decorated with frescoes in a Neo-Gothic style reproducing the coats of arms of the *podestà* who used to live in the building. But in the more distant past the walls of the build-

View of the courtyard

Above: anonymous Florentine artist (14-15th cent.) Scene from the Life of Antonio di Giuseppe Rinaldeschi, *detail with the man hanged from a window of the Bargello Museo Stibbert*

Below: the Verone

ing were covered with pictures of hostile communes or political adversaries, painted by famous artists. These included images of members of the Albizzi, Peruzzi, and Strozzi families depicted on the orders of Cosimo the Elder, as well as those of the Pazzi, portrayed at the time of their conspiracy against the Medici seigniory, Vasari tells us, by Andrea del Castagno. Under Medici rule, at a time when hopes of communal freedom had faded, the building housed (1574) the captain of the guards. The equivalent of the head of police, he was known as the *bargello*, and this is where the building got its present name. Later it was used solely as a prison and this is the reason for the progressive disfigurement of its original elegant ap-

pearance. The grand salons were subdivided into different floors and converted into many small cells. The open galleries were walled up, the fine mural decorations were whitewashed, and the Bargello entered the saddest period in its history (thirty-two cells on four levels were created in what had once been the Hall of the Great Council and now houses the works of Donatello, while the Chapel of the Magdalen was split into two stories).

As a result numerous interventions have been necessary to restore the original appearance of the building, which has now become the most important museum of medieval and Renaissance sculpture and minor arts in Italy. It was Grand Duke Pietro Leopoldo of Lorraine who took the

first step toward reversing the building's decline in the second half of the eighteenth century, by ordering that the instruments of torture still stored in it be burned; later on, in 1857, the prison facilities were moved to a new home in the former convent of the Murate. In this way the original architectural spaces were gradually recovered. The work of restoration was carried out over the course of a century, up until the opening of the museum, in 1865, on the occasion of the celebrations to commemorate the six hundredth anniversary of Dante's birth. The museum was created at a time when there was much interest in the past throughout Europe: it suffices to think of two other great European museums set up along similar archeological lines in that period, the Musée de Cluny in France and the South Kensington Museum in London (now the Victoria and Albert Museum).

The suppression of ecclesiastical bodies that took place following unification of the country enriched the Bargello with substantial collections of sacred objects, while other precious material came from the Uffizi, the Sacristy of the Baptistery, and the Guardaroba in Palazzo Vecchio. Further fundamental contributions were made with the acquisition of entire private collections. These included the rich donation by the French antiquarian Louis Carrand (1888), who left his precious medieval and Renaissance objects to Florence on condition they be put on show in the Bargello. So the range of the collections were expanded just two years after the Bargello had been recognized as a museum of sculpture, on the occasion of the fifth centenary of the birth of Donatello (1886). This bequest was later supplemented by Costantino Ressman's donation of antique weapons (1894) and Giulio Franchetti's one of textiles (1907) Today, as a consequence, the exhibition halls, in addition to evoking ancient stories of violence and torture, create an impression of extreme variety, in which the masterpieces of Florentine sculpture displayed in a medieval setting stand alongside examples of rare objects, providing an unending source of delight to the curious visitor.

The Cappella
della Maddalena

Above:
the Verrocchio Room

Pages 64-65:
Giuseppe Zocchi
The Palazzo del Bargello
from Piazza San Firenze
Property of the Cassa di
Risparmio di Firenze

Tino di Camaino
(Siena ca. 1285 – Naples 1337)
■ *Madonna and Child*
Hall of Medieval Sculpture
marble, ht. 78 cm

This marble statue, one of the most
important examples of fourteenth-century
sculpture in the museum, comes from the
sepulchral monument of Bishop Orso
(whose statue is now in the Museo dell'Opera
del Duomo), which used to be located in
Florence Cathedral. The group depicting the
Madonna and Child was part of the tomb,
probably located at its summit to judge by
the proportions, which only fully make sense
when viewed from below. The inscription on
the base dates from a more recent period,
when the fragment was chosen as the emblem
of Florence University. The elegance of the
Gothic drapery is combined with a more
vigorous handling of space, attained in part
through study of the muscular tensions that
show through the clothing, an anticipation of
the classical revival
that took place
in the fifteenth
century.

Michelangelo Buonarroti
(Caprese, Arezzo, 1475 – Rome 1564)
■ *Pitti Tondo*
Hall of Sixteenth-Century Sculpture
marble, diam. 80 cm

This work is an early masterpiece by
Michelangelo, who carved it at the beginning
of the sixteenth century (1504-5). It takes its
name from the man who commissioned it,
Bartolomeo Pitti, a member of the family of
Florentine bankers who had commenced
construction of the palace in the suburbs that
was later to become the grand ducal residence.
In the fifteenth and sixteenth centuries, tondi
depicting sacred images were used chiefly for
the purposes of private devotion. They could
be painted as well as carved, like the famous
one that Michelangelo himself had executed
for the Doni family and which can now be
seen in the Uffizi.

In relation to fifteenth-century sculptures
influenced by classical art, this work
presents new aspects in the composition of
the figures. This is powerful and yet
harmonious, modulated at various levels of
relief as if to break through the limits
imposed by the material: the strong
projection of the Madonna's face is
combined with the barely accented relief of
the angel, carved using the Donatellian
technique of *schiacciato*. This juxtaposition
of smooth and rough surfaces, and of
different thicknesses of material, strengthens
the contrast between luministic effects and
gives the bas-relief an impression of
mutability.

Michelangelo

■ *Bacchus*

Hall of Sixteenth-Century Sculpture
marble, ht. 207 cm

A juvenile work, it was carved in 1496 to be
set up, along with a number of ancient statues,
in the courtyard of the Palazzo della
Cancelleria in Rome, residence of Cardinal
Riario. The sculpture was not to the cardinal's
liking, perhaps because Michelangelo's
meditations on classical art appeared to have
resulted in a softness and sensuality that he
considered insufficiently virile. So it passed to
a banker, Jacopo Galli, who erected it in the
garden of his villa, until, prompted by Vasari's
praise of the work, the Medici decided to
acquire it for the Uffizi in 1570. Vasari was
greatly impressed by the successful blending of
the muscular energy of a young male with the
fullness and roundness of the female body.

possessed a masterpiece, decided to donate it to Cosimo de' Medici. The work was set up in the grand ducal apartments, where it was admired and imitated by the sculptors of the day. It was transferred from the Uffizi to the Bargello when the decision to create a museum of sculpture was taken in the nineteenth century.

Michelangelo
■ *Brutus*
Hall of Sixteenth-Century Sculpture
marble, ht. 96 cm
The commission for the *Brutus* had political overtones, connected with the theme of tyrannicide. In fact it was carved, between 1539 and 1540, for Cardinal Ridolfi, a member of the party opposed to Medici rule, and was intended as a justification of the recent assassination (1536) of Duke Alessandro de' Medici by his cousin Lorenzo, through allusion to an illustrious precedent in history. Notwithstanding the work's origin, Grand Duke Francesco I de' Medici recognized its high quality and bought it for his Villa di Petraia, from where it was later moved to the Uffizi. For a long time the rough surface of the face – an example of Michelangelo's technique of *non-finito*, or deliberately leaving the sculpture unfinished – was explained away in court circles by the artist's desire to bring out the negative side of Brutus's character.

Jacopo Tatti, called Sansovino
(Florence 1486 – Venice 1570)
■ *Bacchus*
Hall of Sixteenth-Century Sculpture
marble, ht. 146 cm
The comparison with Michelangelo's statue of the same subject is inevitable, given that both of them are on show in the hall on the ground floor of the Bargello, one of the oldest rooms in the building and now used for the display of important works of sixteenth-century Tuscan sculpture. The mobility and elegant tension that characterize Michelangelo's *Bacchus* are nowhere to be seen in this nude with classical proportions. At the time he carved it, Sansovino had just returned from Rome, where he had been working on the restoration of the ancient statues in the papal collection, on show in the Belvedere courtyard. And this work, commissioned by the Florentine merchant Giovanni Bartolini, clearly bears the stamp of his profound reflections on classical antiquity.
On Bartolini's death his heirs, aware that they

Benvenuto Cellini (Florence 1500 – 1571)

■ *Bust of Cosimo I*

Hall of Sixteenth-Century Sculpture

bronze, ht. 110 cm

This is perhaps the finest of Cellini's works in the Bargello, and the grand duke's refined cuirass clearly reveals the artist's origins as a goldsmith and skilled engraver. Worked with great delicacy as if it were a piece of jewelry, it used to be finished with touches of gold, barely visible today, while the irises of Cosimo's eyes were enameled. As the artist himself declares, it was his first work cast in bronze (ca. 1548), but did not meet with the approval of the grand duke, who confined it to the entrance of the Medicean fortress at Portoferraio (Island of Elba). Later it was brought back to the Uffizi and then moved to the museum of sculpture when this was founded.

Benvenuto Cellini

■ *Perseus*
Hall of Sixteenth-Century Sculpture
bronze, ht. 85 cm
This model, like the one in wax that can also
be seen in the Bargello, was made as a
preparatory study for the famous statue of
Perseus under the Loggia dei Lanzi in Piazza
della Signoria. Cellini had worked tirelessly on
the project from 1545 to 1555: it is believed
that, after a series of small bronzes had been
made, this well-shaped and carefully finished
one in the Bargello was the final model
submitted to the grand duke for approval.

It comes from the collection of Eleonora of
Toledo, who used it as a decoration for a
drinking fountain used to dispense wine at
the table.

Jean de Boulogne, called Giambologna
(Douai 1529 – Florence 1608)
■ *Mercury*
Hall of Sixteenth-Century Sculpture
bronze, ht. 170 cm
This is one of the best-known works by the
Flemish sculptor Jean de Boulogne, who chose
to live and work in the Florence of Cosimo I.

It was in fact the grand duke who
commissioned this small bronze, in 1564,
for the wedding of his son Francesco to Joan
of Austria.
Breaking with the traditional iconography in
which the figure is represented in the act of
running, the artist chose to create an
impression of upward movement in a flight of
pure Mannerist virtuosity.
The Museo del Bargello contains a rich
selection of this sculptor's works.

Italian craftwork of the 4-5th century

■ Diptych representing *Adam in the Garden of Eden* and *Scenes from the Life of Saint Paul*
Hall of Ivories
ivory, 29.5x13.6 cm (each panel)
Although the two panels, both of which come from Mainz, are similar in size and were carved around the same time, they have stylistic differences that show they were made by two different artists. In the one on the right, Adam is represented giving names to the animals in the Garden of Eden, recognizable by the four rivers flowing from the rocks that are mentioned in *Genesis*. Amidst this crowd of animals, Adam looks like the mythological figure of Orpheus. In the panel depicting *Scenes from the Life of Saint Paul* on the other hand, the space is split into two levels and recalls the arrangement of Roman bas-reliefs. Here the composition of the figures is less skilled.

Byzantine craftwork of the 6th century

■ *Imperial Diptych*

Hall of Ivories

ivory, 30.5x13.6 cm

This too is a fine specimen from the Carrand collection of ivories, displayed in its entirety (265 pieces) in this room.

The sumptuous dress and regal attributes of the figure suggest that the person portrayed in this fragment of a diptych is one of two empresses, either Amalasuntha or Ariadne. The latter was the widow of Zeno and married Anastasius in 491. The work may have been set inside four plaquettes, judging by the grooves along the edges. These portable diptychs, often depicting sovereigns, must have been used to diffuse the cult of veneration of the emperor.

Parisian craftwork of the 14th century

■ *Carrand Diptych*

Carrand Room

panels, 90x29 cm (each)

This is a refined example of International Gothic, striking for the meticulous detail of the scenes painted on a gold ground and the complexity of the frame of gilded fretwork, where figures of saints can be glimpsed, in a dense and tight rhythm, among the rampant arches and spires. The quality of this portable altar, intended for private devotion, suggests that it was commissioned by a nobleman, perhaps Charles V of Valois, as a wedding gift to his daughter.

Francesco di Giorgio Martini

(Siena 1439 – 1502)

■ *Scipio the African*

Carrand Room

panel, 108x51 cm

The painting hangs in the Carrand Room, which contains the greater part of the Carrand collection, made up of enamelwork, cameos, sacred objects in gold and silver, furniture, and scientific instruments of great value.

The picture belongs to a series of portraits of illustrious men painted by the most important Sienese artists of the time, now split up among the great museums of the world. Commissioned in 1494 as a wedding gift, it was intended to bring honor to its recipients through the representation of personages celebrated for their gifts and virtues. The panel illustrates the magnanimity of Scipio, who refuses Lucretia as a spoil of war and restores her to her betrothed.

Parisian craftwork of the 15th century

■ *Brooch with dromedary*

Carrand Room

gold, enamel, pearls, diam. 5 cm

Decorations of this type were pinned or sewn onto clothing. The skilled craftsmen who made them often took their ideas from

illuminations and the decorative motifs of fabrics or pottery. This is a typical example: plant motifs or geometric patterns framing a fantastic or exotic animal.

French craftwork of the 9th century

■ *Flabellum of Tournus*

Hall of Ivories

ivory, bone, metal, parchment, ht. 78 cm

This is one of the rarest and most precious objects from the Carrand collection and a testimony to the curious and eclectic interests of its generous owner. It is a refined example, in which even the painted parchment is well-preserved, of a flabellum, a fan that was used during religious services to drive away insects from the chalices and sacred drinks. It has three parts: the fan itself, a case, and a handle. It was made around 845 for the monks of Saint-Philibert, in France.

Longobard craftwork of the 6th century

■ *Decoration of Agilulf's helmet*

Carrand Room

gilded bronze, 7.4x18 cm

We know that it was used as the visor of the helmet worn by the Longobard king Agilulf from the inscription: DN AGILU REGI. It was found during excavations in Valdinievole and has been in the Bargello since 1891. It is embossed with the coronation of the king, depicted in the schematic manner typical of medieval art.

Florentine craftwork of the 16th century

■ *Hunting horn*
Carrand Room
buffalo horn, bronze, wood
This refined instrument of Florentine manufacture, used for hunting, comes from the Medici collections.

German craftwork of the 15th century

■ Ewer decorated with *Saint George and the Dragon*
Carrand Room
bronze, 41x36.2 cm
Ewers were objects, generally in the shape of an animal, used to serve water at table. This one represents St. George killing the dragon as it clambers up the hind leg of his horse. The twisted figure is particularly lively and depicted with the elegance of a skilled chaser. The showcase also contains precious examples of German craftwork from an earlier period, like the one illustrated on the right (ca. 1250).

French craftwork of the 16th century

■ *Moneybag*
Carrand Room
leather, metal, embroidery
Another example of the kind of curiosity to be found in the museum. It is a moneybag, worn by men in the fourteenth and fifteenth century and attached to the belt by a metal ring. It usually had a complicated shape and pockets decorated with lace and embroidery. One can be seen in the painting of the *Moneychanger* on view in the same room.

Giovanni di Francesco
(Florence 1412 – documented before 1459)
■ *Madonna and Child with Saints*
Cappella della Maddalena
panel, 182x163 cm
This triptych, which may have been
commissioned for the church of San Niccolò,
was painted by Giovanni di Francesco, known
as "Cervelliera," a Florentine artist from the
mid fifteenth century who was influenced by
fourteenth-century works on a gold ground
and yet open to the experimentation with
perspective carried out by such innovative
artists as Paolo Uccello and Domenico
Veneziano. The work was part of the Carrand
collection and is now displayed in the space
that originally housed the altar of the chapel
of the Magdalen.
It should be pointed out that the chapel,
decorated with frescoes by the school of
Giotto, was restored to its original state in the
nineteenth century, after the drastic structural
alterations made in the Medicean period. It is
now used for the display of sacred objects in
gold and silver that recall its original function.

Antonio di Salvi
■ *"Pace" decorated with the Deposition*
Cappella della Maddalena
silver, enamel
The showcases in the chapel of the Magdalen
hold sacred ornaments and objects of exquisite

workmanship from churches in Florence. This
pace, made by Antonio di Salvi, is a kind of
platen that the officiant of the Mass gave
worshipers to kiss at the moment of the *Agnus
Dei*. An elegant composition in embossed
silver, with polychrome enamelwork, it has the
typical forms of Florentine architectural
decoration. The animated drapery and curly
heads of hair of the two praying angels show
the influence of Donatello's sculpture.

Antonio Benci, called **Antonio del
Pollaiolo** (Florence 1431 – Rome 1498)
and **unknown silversmith of the first
half of the 16th century**
■ *Reliquary cross*
Cappella della Maddalena
gilded and chased copper, enamel plaquettes
on silver, 57x48.8 cm
One of the most beautiful examples of the
silversmith's art in the chapel, it is the work of
a famous artist, Antonio del Pollaiolo. It was
commissioned from him by the monastery of
San Gaggio and made between 1476 and
1483. The six enamel and silver plaquettes are,
unfortunately, all that remains of the original,
as the cross has been lost and replaced by a
later one. The intense expressiveness created
by the lively combination of enamelwork and
silver is typical of the Florentine artist's style.

Donatello

■ *Saint George*
Donatello Room
marble, ht. 209 cm
In 1415 the Guild of Armorers and
Swordsmiths commissioned the sculptor to
carve a niche with a statue of St. George,
patron of the guild, for the exterior of the
church of Orsanmichele. The resolute quality
of Donatello's sculpture is clearly apparent in
this celebrated work. The balance of forms
and forces with which the *Saint George* is
constructed is certainly based on the study of
ancient statuary, but it is handled with a
naturalness and energy that are typical of the
Renaissance, with sharp contrasts of light and
shade that almost bring the marble to life.
Even the scene depicted on the base is

Donato di Niccolò di Betto Bardi,
called **Donatello** (Florence 1386 – 1466)
■ *David*
Donatello Room
marble, ht. 191 cm
On the occasion of the centenary of the birth
of Donatello, in 1886, a major exhibition
marked the definitive consecration of this
room to the great master and to other
important Florentine sculptors of the fifteenth
century. It houses the largest collection of
Donatello's sculptures in the world.

The marble statue of *David* is an early work
by the artist, in which the body's graceful and
flexible attitude echoes the Gothic elegance of
Ghiberti, while the odd daring touch already
hints at a more solid and imposing style of
sculpture: the hands vibrant with taut sinews,
the intense and resolute gaze. It was carved as
a companion to Nanni di Banco's *Isaiah* for
the apsidal spurs of Santa Maria del Fiore, but
was never put in place. In 1416 it was set up
in Palazzo Vecchio as a symbol and model of
heroic virtue.

innovative in character: the artist breaks with the tradition of the bas-relief through masterly use of a technique, known as *schiacciato*, that allows him to represent space in perspective by a subtle gradation of planes and attain results similar to those of painting. In 1892, to the disappointment of all, the statue was removed from its niche and placed in the Bargello for reasons of conservation.

Donatello
■ *David*
Donatello Room
bronze, ht. 158 cm
The subject of this famous work by Donatello is open to doubt. It has recently been interpreted as a *David-Mercury*, since the young man, naked except for a hat, does not follow the traditional iconography for David, the symbol of republican freedom in Florence. It was made at the time of Lorenzo the Magnificent's marriage to Clarice Orsini and erected in the courtyard of Palazzo Medici. It was removed from there at the time of the establishment of the republic and set up in Palazzo Vecchio (1494). This was when the sculpture was identified as representing David, but the elegant young man shows none of the resoluteness of his marble rival standing just outside the palace. Its harmonious forms seem more suited to the representation of a Greek god.

Donatello
■ *Atys*
Donatello Room
bronze, ht. 104 cm
There have been a plethora of suggestions as to the subject of this small figure by Donatello that Vasari claims to have seen in the house of a wealthy Florentine, Giovan Battista d'Agnolo Doni, but which was long thought to be an Etruscan sculpture. It was presumably executed between 1430 and 1440. Doubts have been raised about the curious position of the arms that make it a dancing figure, as joins are visible at the point of attachment, which may date from later. Traces of lost attributes that might have helped in identification of the subject can be seen in the hands.

Donatello
▪ *Niccolò da Uzzano*
Donatello Room
polychrome terra-cotta, ht. 46 cm
Among the marbles and bronzes by Donatello on show in the hall that used to be the chamber of the Grand Council when the building was the residence of the *podestà*, this portrait of an illustrious Florentine Humanist and military leader of the time stands out for its marked realism, accentuated by the naturalistic use of color. His robust and terse features must have attracted many artists, for Masaccio portrayed him in a fresco in the Carmelite Church that has been lost and we can still recognize his face in Benozzo Gozzoli's *Journey of the Magi* in the chapel of Palazzo Medici-Riccardi.

Luca della Robbia (Florence 1400 – 1482)
▪ *Madonna della Mela*
Donatello Room
glazed terra-cotta, 67x51 cm
Luca della Robbia's principal claim to fame lies in having been the first to apply a specially developed tin-based glaze to terra-cotta sculpture. This vitrified glaze, called *invetriatura* in Italian, was the "great secret" of the Della Robbia workshop. Luca, his nephew Andrea, and Andrea's son Giovanni were the leading lights in this highly unusual aspect of the Florentine artistic scene. In a collection with no parallel elsewhere in the world, the Museo del Bargello has important works by all of them.

The *Madonna della Mela* (*Madonna of the Apple*) was commissioned by the Medici in 1460 and then placed by them in the Uffizi, from where it was transferred to the Bargello. The shimmering reflections of the light from the glazed terra-cotta enlivens the Madonna's gaze, which shows similarities to those of Donatello's figures. The softness of the lines – note the gracefulness of the hand that is delicately clasping the Child's thigh – is reminiscent of Ghiberti.

Lorenzo Ghiberti (Florence 1378 – 1455)
Filippo Brunelleschi (Florence 1377 – 1446)
▪ *Sacrifice of Isaac*
Donatello Room
gilded bronze, 44x40 cm; 47x40 cm
The two panels depict the same subject because they were both made for the famous competition held in 1402 for the second door of Florence Baptistery. Ghiberti won the competition, with a panel that earned fulsome praise from Vasari, who declared that it

showed "design, diligence, individuality, craftsmanship." In fact the skill of the practiced goldsmith is apparent in the treatment of the clothes and the altar on which the sacrifice is being made, along with the influence of the classical art especially in the harmonious nude figure of Isaac. Brunelleschi's panel, on the other hand, has a much more animated appearance, filled with diagonals and forces that try to break out of the limits of the mixtilinear frame, imposed by the terms of the competition. The height of drama is reached in the pyramidal composition by the tragic gesture of the father and the contrasting one of the delivering angel.

Brunelleschi donated the rejected panel to Cosimo the Elder, while even Ghiberti's did not find a place on the baptistery doors because the commission decided to have him decorate them with scenes from the New Testament instead of the Old. So the guild known as the Corporazione di Calimala placed it in its own audience chamber.

Giovanni di Francesco Toscani
(1370 - ca. 1430)
■ *Chest of the Standards*
Donatello Room
painted wood, 62x193x66 cm

The display in this room is completed by a number of chests, typical furnishings in the bedchambers of noble houses that were used to store the mistress's trousseau. They were decorated with scenes of a profane character. The example painted by Giovanni Toscani represents the parade of pallia – tall standards decorated with the coats of arms of the quarters and guilds of the city that were carried in procession – that was staged between Piazza della Signoria and the Baptistery. On the sides of the chest, family coats of arms and portraits of the bride and groom commemorate the clients and the marriage for which the work was commissioned.

Giambologna
■ *Turkey; Eagle*
Verone
bronze, 62x50 cm; 50.5x83.2 cm
A letter referring to these and other sculptures of animals made by the artist for Francesco I de' Medici, the eccentric grand duke who had the Studiolo built in Palazzo Vecchio, allows us to date them to 1567. The ones now in the Bargello are just a few examples from the series of bronze birds executed for the garden of the Medici Villa di Castello. They are kept in the *Verone*, the fourteenth-century loggia facing onto the courtyard. The artist shows admirable skill in conveying the temperament of the different creatures with great realism. Thus we see the haughty *turkey*, then a new species imported from America, and the *eagle*, the bird of prey poised on a rock, with an alert and rapacious gaze.

Francesco Xanto Avelli da Rovigo
(? – Urbino 1545)
■ Dish with *Joseph fleeing from Potiphar's Wife*
Majolica Room
Majolica, diam. 45 cm
This plate made by a craftsman active in the circles of the Della Rovere family, in the early years of the sixteenth century, is a fine example of the collection of majolica ware based on the large number of such pieces in the grand ducal collections and which was later enriched by the bequests of modern collectors such as Carrand. This plate, signed and dated 1537, represents the biblical scene in the style of Raphael, the artist from whom the potter usually drew his inspiration.

Urbino pottery of the 16th century
■ Cooler depicting *Hannibal crossing the Alps*
Majolica Room
Majolica, diam. 51 cm, ht. 23.5 cm
The Medici family's interest in pottery led them to collect objects made not only at Faenza and Deruta, but also at the factory in Urbino, which underwent a notable flowering in the sixteenth century. It is from that period that this tub-cooler dates. It was kept by Francesco I in the Casino Mediceo di San Marco along with other ceramic furnishings that are now in the Bargello.

Faenza pottery of the 16th century
■ Goblet decorated with the *Triumph of the Moon*
Majolica Room
Majolica, diam. 33 cm
The "Master of Selene" who made this fine example of "bianco di Faenza" – as the pottery of this sixteenth-century school was called – took his name from just this representation of the *Triumph of the Moon*, at the center of the bowl, in blue monochrome on a white ground. The polychrome decoration of the molding has a motif of panoplies of classical inspiration.

Pastorino Pastorini (Castelnuovo Berardenga 1508 – Florence 1592)
■ Medallion with *Bust of Francesco I*
Majolica Room
pottery, ht. 12.8 cm

The author of this elegant plaque with a portrait of the grand duke was a medalist of Sienese origin, who worked for the Medici family from 1576 until his death. Francesco I is depicted in profile and in noble dress. The initials of the artist's name are inscribed on the puff of the sleeve.

Giovanni della Robbia
(Florence 1469 – 1529)
■ *Crib*
Giovanni della Robbia Room
glazed terra-cotta, 280x155 cm
The first room you come to on the top floor of the museum houses works by Giovanni della Robbia, Luca's grandnephew, and his workshop. They are not always of the highest quality, partly because they were mass produced and showed little variation, yet they still include a number of fine works, such as the *Noli me tangere* modeled by Giovan Francesco Rustici and then glazed by Giovanni della Robbia on a golden yellow ground, or this *Crib* (1521), rich in figures and colors, from the church of San Girolamo delle Poverine.

Andrea della Robbia
(Florence 1435 – 1525)
■ *Portrait of an Unknown Girl*
Andrea della Robbia Room
glazed terra-cotta, diam. 49 cm

This portrait of a girl by Andrea della Robbia (Giovanni's father and Luca's nephew) can be dated to 1470. It is reminiscent of similar portraits in marble by fifteenth-century sculptors, from Desiderio da Settignano to the Rossellino brothers, whose works can be seen in the adjoining room. These artists typically portrayed young women with thin faces and long and graceful necks, and these characteristics are accentuated in this work in high relief.
There is another delicate *Bust of a Boy* (1475) on show in this room.

German craftwork of the 17th century

■ *Armor worn by Cosimo III as a child*
Hall of Arms
chased and engraved steel, gilt
This is one of the most curious exhibits in the Bargello's collection of arms. It was worn by Cosimo III de' Medici when he took part in parades as a child, and was later passed on to his son Ferdinando. There are many other valuable pieces in the Medicean collection, such as helms, trimmings, horse armor, and hunting horns (including one that may well have belonged to Lorenzo the Magnificent), that have survived in spite of the looting that took place during the numerous political upheavals. Then at the end of the eighteenth century, in the new climate of reform introduced by Leopoldo II, it was decided to select the finest pieces and melt down the rest, with the result that the roughly 9500 pieces that had been in the collection the previous century were reduced to 856. Today these are on display along with others from donations to the museum, in particular the Ressmann one of 1899.

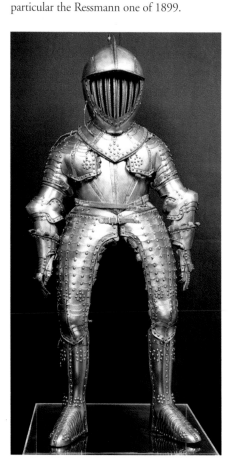

Antonio Pollaiolo

■ *Hercules and Antaeus*
Hall of Bronzes
bronze, ht. 45 cm
The remarkable number of small bronzes on display in this room are indicative of the great interest in this art form shown by the Medici family and by sixteenth-century collectors in general. The greater part of the collection comes from the Uffizi, with the addition of examples from Palazzo Pitti, the Guardaroba in Palazzo Vecchio, and the Carrand collection. One of the finest is this lively group by Antonio del Pollaiolo, an example of his skill as a goldsmith and his study of ancient art. He had already depicted the same theme in a painting, now in the Uffizi, but perhaps because of its three-dimensionality and the effect of light on the bronze, this new version (1475) shows a greater interest in the representation of muscular strength.

Benvenuto Cellini

■ *Greyhound*
Hall of Bronzes
bronze, 18x27.8 cm
Benvenuto Cellini mentions this work in his
Trattati, claiming that it was commissioned by
Grand Duke Cosimo I as a trial for a much
more demanding undertaking, that of the
celebrated bronze figure of *Perseus* in the
Loggia dei Lanzi. And in fact there are points
of similarity between the base of that sculpture
and this *Greyhound*, where the artist has
produced a masterly blend of full relief and
parts in very low relief
(*schiacciato*).

Giambologna

■ *The Dwarf Morgante*
Hall of Bronzes
bronze, ht. 36.5 cm
The chubby features of Morgante, the dwarf
jester of the Medici family who was portrayed
several times by court artists, stimulated the
lively imagination of Giambologna, who
represents him absorbed in fishing, seated on
the back of a dragon (executed by the
goldsmith Vincenzo della Nera). Made for
Francesco I in the years 1582-83, the small
bronze was intended to complete the fountain
set on the terrace of the Uffizi above the
Loggia dei Lanzi.

Ludovico Cardi, called Cigoli
(Castelvecchio di Cigoli, Florence,
1559 – Rome 1613)
■ *The Flayed Man*
Hall of Bronzes
bronze, ht. 65 cm
The Flayed Man, of which the Bargello also
has the wax model, is the work of a Florentine
painter of the Counter Reformation and
is indicative of seventeenth-century interest in
the accurate study of anatomy. Both wax and
bronze aroused the interest of artists and
intellectuals.
It comes from the Uffizi, which it entered in
the eighteenth century, after changing hands
many times.

Francesco Laurana
(Zadar ca. 1430 – Avignon? 1502)
■ *Battista Sforza*
Verrocchio Room
marble, ht. 50 cm
The lines of this exalted representation of the
consort of Federico da Montefeltro, duke of
Urbino, are extremely terse. The portrait
shows a remarkable similarity to the one
painted by Piero della Francesca, now in the
Uffizi, which seems to have influenced
Laurana's bust even in its modulation of light.
The work was brought to Florence by
Ferdinando II's wife, Vittoria della Rovere of
Urbino, whose dowry added many
masterpieces to the Medici collections.

Andrea di Francesco di Cione,
called **Verrocchio**
(Florence 1435 – Venice 1488)
■ *Noblewoman with Nosegay*
Verrocchio Room
marble, ht. 57 cm
At the time the sculpture entered the museum
it was attributed to Donatello. It is now
unanimously recognized to be the work of
Verrocchio, although there are those who like
to see, in the beautiful detail of the hands and
the fine naturalism of the whole, an
intervention by the young Leonardo, then an
apprentice in the artist's workshop.
The woman portrayed has sometimes been
identified as Ginevra Benci (because of the
resemblance to Leonardo's celebrated portrait),
or as another Florentine lady, Lucrezia Donati,
friend of Lorenzo the Magnificent.

Verrocchio

■ *David*

Verrocchio Room

bronze, ht. 120 cm

The third masterpiece depicting David to be found in the Museo del Bargello is the work of Verrocchio, to whom the room containing works of Tuscan sculpture from the second half of the fifteenth century is dedicated. While the hero *par excellence*, so dear to Renaissance culture, does seem to display pride in his valorous deed, he has been transfigured by an ideal of grace and beauty that strips the figure of any symbolic dimension. The statue was sold (1476) by the Medici – who had commissioned it for the Villa di Careggi – to the Signoria and set up at the entrance of the Sala dei Gigli in Palazzo Vecchio, where it remained until the seventeenth century.

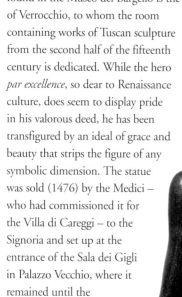

Mino da Fiesole

(Poppi 1429 – Florence 1484)

■ *Piero de' Medici*

Verrocchio Room

marble, ht. 54 cm

The subject is Piero "the Gouty," father of the more famous Lorenzo the Magnificent. He is portrayed here above alongside many other Florentines of his day – including the extremely wealthy merchant Pietro Mellini (below) – in a room that houses one of the most extensive collections of Renaissance sculpted portraiture in existence. The style of these busts recalls their ancient Roman prototypes, but they also seem to show a constant preoccupation with the accurate representation of features that derives from Flemish influences.

Gian Lorenzo Bernini
(Naples 1598 – Rome 1680)
■ *Costanza Bonarelli*
Medal Rooms
marble, ht. 70 cm

The nineteenth-century cases in the medal rooms, arranged in chronological order and by schools, are interspersed with valuable bronzes and marbles from the seventeenth century. One of the finest of these baroque works is the portrait of Costanza Bonarelli, carved by Bernini in 1635. The artist emphasizes the woman's confident and strong-willed gaze, an impression that is strengthened by the soft head of hair constructed with great skill and the thin and delicate drapery of her disheveled clothes.

Antonio Pisano, called Pisanello
(Pisa ca. 1380 – Mantua? by 1455)
■ Medal representing *Lionello d'Este*
Medal Rooms
bronze, diam. 6.7 cm

This medal belongs to the oldest section of the Medicean collection once housed in the Uffizi. This genre was very popular in the fifteenth century, and had a commemorative function similar to that of medals in the Roman era. Lionello's profile was a celebrated one and portrayed several times in paintings as well. It served as a model for Matteo de' Pasti, author of the medals with profiles of members of the Malatesta family, on display in the same room.

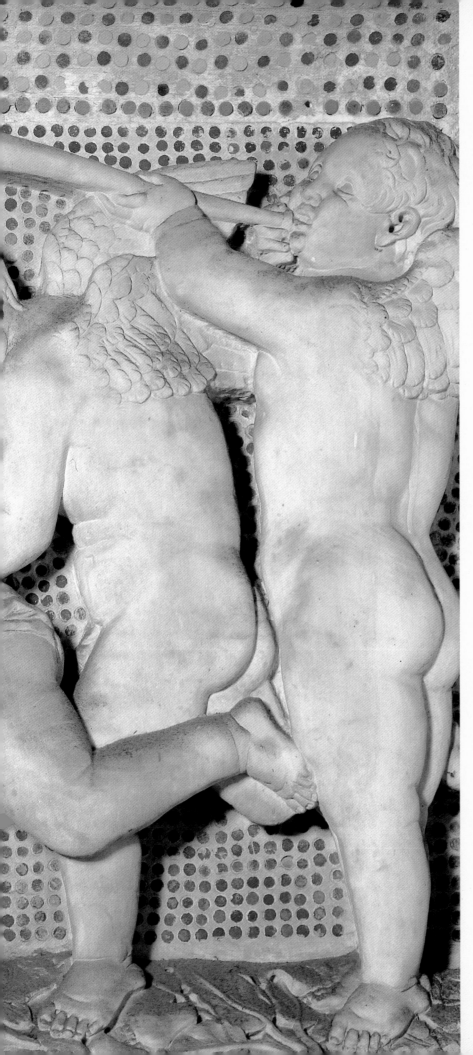

MUSEO DELL'OPERA DEL DUOMO

The majestic cathedral of Florence has a long and fascinating history. Significant testimonies to this history can be found in the Museo dell'Opera del Duomo, the Museum of the Cathedral Vestry Board. The entrance to the museum is located on the north side of the cathedral square – opposite the apse of the cathedral – in a building that used to house the Magistratura dell'Opera, or Board of Trustees of the Cathedral, at the beginning of the fifteenth century. This ancient institution was responsible for overseeing the work of construction of the new cathedral and had enjoyed the patronage of the Wool Guild ever since 1331.

For several centuries the building served another and no less important function, that of housing, or storing for a limited period, sculptures destined for the cathedral or works removed from it as a result of changes in taste. It was not turned into a true museum, however, until much later, toward the end of the nineteenth century, as a consequence of the renewal of interest in Renaissance sculpture and the art and history of the past in general. Thus the Museo dell'Opera was opened in 1891, with the aim of documenting the story of the city's most glorious monument and providing a permanent and

worthy home for outstanding works of art, such as Donatello and Luca della Robbia's *Cantorie,* or *Singing Galleries,* which had previously been housed in the Uffizi and then the Bargello. So in the 1870s Emilio de Fabris, the architect who had designed the Tribuna of the *David* and the facade of Santa Maria del Fiore itself, was given the task of restoring the seat of the Vestry Board, which no longer, after many alterations, had the original appearance given to it (1432) by its first architect, Filippo Brunelleschi.

At the same time the collection was enriched with valuable works from the baptistery, in virtue of the merger of the Vestry Boards of San Giovanni and the cathedral, along with numerous other pieces that had been scattered round the city and then patiently tracked down. During the first few decades of its life the museum underwent continuous alterations and enlargements as it acquired a series of salvaged materials and sculptures from a variety of religious buildings, from which they were removed to protect them against damage by atmospheric agents and replaced by plaster copies. In the 1960s-70s it assumed a more stable structure and was given a more rational organization that has remained more or less unchanged down to the present day: the ground floor, devoted chiefly to documentation of the facade and the construction of Brunelleschi's dome but also housing collections of illuminations and church ornaments; the second floor, dedicated to the sculptures of the campanile, the *Cantorie,* important works from the baptistery, and a number of paintings removed from the cathedral. In more recent years three more masterpieces have been added to the museum's collection: Donatello's *Magdalen* (in 1972), Michelangelo's *Pietà* (1981), and four of the ten panels from the Door of Paradise (1985), which is still undergoing restoration.

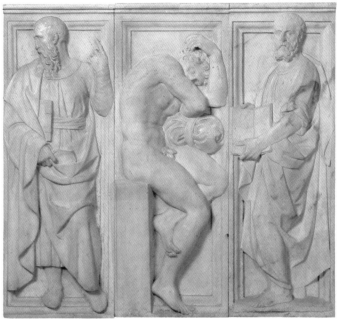

Baccio Bandinelli (Florence 1493 – 1560)
■ Bas-relief with *Nudes, Prophets, and Apostles*
Vestibule
marble, 98x36 cm
In the small room used as a vestibule can be seen, in addition to a significant *Bust of Brunelleschi* attributed to Andrea Cavalcanti, fifteen marble bas-reliefs that are ranged along the walls. Taken from the choir screen of the cathedral, they were commissioned by Cosimo I and are the product of many years' work (1547-72) by Baccio Bandinelli and his pupil Giovanni Bandini.

They are considered the sculptor's masterpiece, free of any academic style and close, in the skillful fluidity of their outlines, to the contemporary paintings of Rosso Fiorentino and Andrea del Sarto.

Bernardino Barbatelli, called **Poccetti**
(Florence 1548 – 1612)
■ *Drawing of the old facade of the cathedral*
Sala dell'antica facciata del Duomo
canvas, 101x58 cm
The vast space known as the Room of the Old Cathedral Facade houses the surviving statues from the facade designed by Arnolfo di Cambio, which was left incomplete and then demolished in 1587. This interesting drawing by Bernardino Poccetti, a painter and decorator of the late sixteenth century, is regarded by scholars as the most reliable source for reconstruction of the original design. In fact the study is carried out with great accuracy and clearly shows the composition of the decoration and the location of the statues. The drawing must have been commissioned from Poccetti by the architect Bernardo Buontalenti, who gave it to the Vestry Board in 1608.

Arnolfo di Cambio
(Colle Val d'Elsa ca. 1245 – Florence 1302)
■ *Madonna and Child*
Sala dell'antica facciata del Duomo
marble, ht. 173 cm
Alongside his role as architect of the new cathedral of Santa Maria del Fiore, which he started to build in 1296, Arnolfo di Cambio also worked as a sculptor. With the help of his active workshop, in fact, he furnished the abundant sculptural decoration called for in the design. This large *Madonna and Child*

formed part of the decoration and was set in the lunette of the central portal. It was flanked by two figures representing *Saint Zenobius*, bishop of Florence, and *Saint Reparata*, patron of the city and titular of the original cathedral, which have been fortuitously recovered and replaced at its sides. The statue, which is also known as the "Madonna with Glass Eyes" owing to the curious insertion of pieces of colored enamel, used to be an object of great popular devotion and was spared destruction for this reason. It still has some of the character of a Byzantine icon, but this is tempered by a fullness of form and a new plastic sense of construction that bring it into line with the handling of volume in Giotto's painting.

Giovanni di Antonio di Banco, called **Nanni di Banco** (Florence 1380/90 – 1421) and **Donato di Niccolò di Betto Bardi**, called **Donatello** (Florence 1386 – 1466)
■ *Saint Luke and Saint John the Evangelist*
Sala dell'antica facciata del Duomo
marble, ht. 207 cm, 212 cm
These are two of the four evangelists that were carved, between 1408 and 1415, by the leading Florentine sculptors of the day (Niccolò Lamberti, Nanni di Banco, Donatello, and Bernardo Ciuffagni) for the niches at the sides of the cathedral's main portal, in accordance with Arnolfo's original design. They were preserved from the demolition of the facade because of their recognized artistic quality and are now presented to visitors, in all their diversity, as a significant cross section of Florentine sculpture

at the beginning of the fifteenth century. From the predominantly Gothic and fairly stiff style of Niccolò Lamberti's *Saint Mark*, there is a shift to the balanced monumentality that Nanni di Banco was able to impart to his *Saint Luke*, represented in a natural pose as if engaged in mute conversation with the observer. Donatello gives his *Saint John*, carved with details of great realism that are a sign of the sculptor's modernity, a quite different attitude. Its most striking features are the hand slipped between the deep folds of the robe and the frowning expression, whose intensity seems to have provided the inspiration for Michelangelo's *Moses*. But it must also have inspired Ciuffagni who, though achieving very different results from Donatello, has left us one of his finest works in the *Saint Matthew*.

Michelangelo Buonarroti
(Caprese, Arezzo, 1475 – Rome 1564)
■ *Pietà*
Mezzanine
marble, ht. 226 cm
Sometimes called the *Bandini Pietà*, it is the most famous work in the museum. A whole room is dedicated to it and, though small in size, allows the work to be seen from various angles.
Michelangelo's contemporary biographers say that the sculpture was carved in the artist's maturity (1550-55) for the mortuary chapel he designed for himself in Santa Maria Maggiore at Rome. He may have been prompted to think of his own end by the recent death (1547) of a close friend, Vittoria Colonna. Dissatisfied with the work, or perhaps thwarted by flaws in the marble, he stopped working on the statue in 1555, after having tried to destroy it. It was then acquired by a Florentine sculptor, Francesco Bandini, who gave it to one of Michelangelo's pupils, Tiberio Calcagni, to repair and finish. Using Michelangelo's designs, Calcagni completed the figure of the Magdalen and the left leg of Christ. The sculpture remained for a long time in the garden of Bandini's house in Rome. It only came to Florence when it was bought by Grand Duke Cosimo III, who placed it in the crypt of San Lorenzo, from where it was moved to the cathedral. In 1981 it was transferred, amidst fierce arguments, to the Museo dell'Opera del Duomo.
Although Michelangelo repudiated the sculpture, there can be no doubt that much of the group bears the stamp of his genius, and it has elements in common with such late works as the *Rondanini Pietà* in the Castello Sforzesco at Milan. Vasari recognized the bearded old man that surmounts the group, perhaps representing the Nicodemus mentioned in the Gospel according to John, as a self-portrait of the elderly artist.

Andrea da Pontedera, called **Andrea Pisano** (Pontedera ca. 1290 – Orvieto after 1348) and **Luca della Robbia** (Florence 1400 – 1482)

■ *Sculpture, Logic* and *Dialectics*
Sala delle formelle del Campanile
Marble, 83x69 cm (each)

As its name suggests, the Room of the Campanile Panels contains part of the decorations (panels and statues) that used to adorn Giotto's campanile but which were removed in the mid sixties for reasons of conservation.

The decoration is a unitary cycle made in the first half of the fourteenth century – to which Giotto himself contributed – and was intended to represent man's journey of redemption from original sin, illustrated in accordance with the doctrines of Scholasticism. The panels, which are arranged on the walls in the same sequence they had on the campanile, were entrusted with the task of representing this program, starting from the

creation of man and passing through his progressive civilization by means of various activities to his definitive elevation to the state of salvation through the *Planets* (forces of nature), *Virtues* (moral forces), and *Liberal Arts* (intellectual forces). At the top stood the *Sacraments*, which are the direct means of salvation.

Traditionally, the majority of the reliefs are ascribed to Andrea Pisano, although it is not impossible that Giotto made some contribution. Luca della Robbia carved the five panels depicting the *Liberal Arts*.

Donatello

■ *Jeremiah; Habakkuk*
Sala delle Cantorie
marble, ht. 193 cm, 196 cm

One of the oldest rooms in the museum is used to display, close to the famous *Singing Galleries (Cantorie)*, the sixteen statues that used to decorate the niches of the campanile, carved at different times by Andrea Pisano, Donatello, and Nanni di Bartolo.

Jeremiah and *Habakkuk*, the two prophets that Donatello executed between 1425 and 1436 for the western side of the campanile, stand out for their vitality and intensity of

expression. They are depicted with crude, almost harsh realism, as ascetic figures, their bodies emaciated under their tunics: *Habakkuk* is completely bald, a fact that has earned him the popular nickname of "lo Zuccone" (Pumpkin Head), while *Jeremiah*, the prophet whose fate it was to predict the destruction of Jerusalem, has tight lips and an unkempt beard. Vasari initiated a long tradition by identifying them as portraits of two enemies of the Medici family, the Florentine nobleman Giovanni Cherichini and Francesco Soderini.

Luca della Robbia and **Donatello**
■ *Cantorie*
Sala delle Cantorie
marble, 328x560 cm; 348x570 cm
These formed the two balconies of the organs and were originally set above the doors leading into the sacristy of the cathedral. They remained in this position until 1688, when they were taken down to make room for the decorations set up in the church to celebrate a Medici wedding, between Cosimo III's son and Violante of Bavaria, and never replaced. Today, after a patient work of reassemblage, integration, and restoration, they constitute one of the main attractions of the museum, which, obliged to find a suitable setting, has devoted a large room to them.

Their position opposite one another allows the observer to see them both at once and favors direct comparisons. A sense of monumental classicism imbues Luca's *Cantoria*, which was the first to be commissioned (1431) and carved over a period of eight years. Donatello's, made slightly later (1433-38), is permeated by a modern conception of freedom. The naturalness of pose of the boys harmoniously modeled by della Robbia and distributed over ten panels in two rows contrasts with the irrepressible vitality of Donatello's putti, set against a mosaic background of great inventiveness. Even the space and movement are rendered by different techniques: the execution of the former is elaborate to a degree of compositional perfection, with space represented through a graduation of relief, while Donatello's carving is more immediate and less polished, using a barely sketched relief to obtain masterly effects of depth.

Donatello
■ *Magdalen*
Sala delle Cantorie
wood, ht. 188 cm
Under Donatello's *Cantoria* is set another of his works, the wooden statue of the *Magdalen* that used to be in the baptistery. It is usually associated with other figures of ascetics, in particular the *Saint John the Baptist* in Siena Cathedral, and on this basis, in the absence of documentary evidence, is dated to a late phase of Donatello's career. The features of Mary Magdalene, portrayed in the unusual guise of an old woman who has attained salvation through the very loss of her beauty, are particularly accentuated in order to convey a sense of suffering. Perhaps these dramatic figures can be seen as the artist's personal meditations on old age.

Lorenzo Ghiberti (Florence 1378 – 1455)
■ Panels of the Door of Paradise with *Scenes from the Life of Joseph*
Sala dell'altare d'argento
gilded bronze, 79.5x80 cm
In 1425 Lorenzo Ghiberti, winner of the famous competition held by the Arte della Lana, or Wool Guild, to determine who would receive the commission for the second door of the baptistery, was also entrusted with the task of making the third door, the one opening onto the facade of the cathedral which later came to be known as the "Door of Paradise." Unlike the earlier work, he used a simpler scheme of composition this time, divided up into only ten panels representing scenes from the Old Testament. More than one episode is represented in each panel, following an iconographic program in which the Humanist Leonardo Bruni must have been involved, at least in the early stages.

The scenes teem with figures and are handled with Ghiberti's customary elegance, but they also show that he had taken on board the most recent developments in Renaissance art, from Donatello's technique of *schiacciato*, or extremely low relief, to the experiments with perspective carried out by Brunelleschi and Masaccio.

The door still awaits complete reassemblage in the museum, while the baptistery unfortunately has to make do with a copy, for reasons of conservation.

Florentine craftsmen of the 14th and 15th century

■ *Altar Frontal of San Giovanni*
Sala dell'altare d'argento
silver, enamel, 115x263 cm
In front of the panels of the Door of Paradise, as a reminder of their common origin, is set the precious *Altar Frontal of San Giovanni*, which used to serve as an ornament and protection for the high altar of the baptistery and was later placed over the font, on solemn occasions, when the rich treasure of San Giovanni was put on display.

It was begun in 1367 to a commission from the Arte di Calimala, the patron guild of the baptistery, with the express intention of creating an exceptional work, one that would have no equal in richness and magnificence. Indeed the undertaking proved to be an extremely demanding one and the four lateral reliefs were not completed until over a century later (1480), with the participation of outstanding goldsmiths and sculptors. An elaborate Gothic frame, studded with pinnacles and niches inspired by the decorations of the campanile and the southern

door of the cathedral, surrounds twelve panels depicting scenes from the life of the Baptist. At the center is set a statue of the saint, a sculpture by Michelozzo as precious as it is rare.

On the altar stands the great silver *Cross* (1457-59), also commissioned by the Arte di

Calimala. An elegant piece of sacred silver work, it is the product of a collaboration between several artists, one of whom is certain to have been Antonio del Pollaiolo.

QUI PERVENNE DALLA GROTTA DEL BUONTALENTI
IN BOBOLI NEL LUGLIO 1909

Galleria dell' Accademia

The Galleria dell'Accademia was created in 1784, when Grand Duke Pietro Leopoldo of Lorraine decided to endow the School of Fine Arts, located in the fourteenth-century hospital of San Matteo, with a collection of high-quality works of art. These were to serve as an example to students, who would be able to study and imitate them. At the time, in fact, the activity of copying masterpieces of the past, and especially the Florentine school of the fifteenth and sixteenth century which was thought to have come the closest to perfection of form, was regarded as essential to learning the correct technique. Initially the paintings came from the Medici collections and from the suppression of religious bodies commenced by the grand duke himself and continued in the Napoleonic period and after the creation of the kingdom of Italy.

In the meantime, the rooms used to house the new acquisitions proved insufficient and part of the adjoining building was annexed. This had once been the monastery of San Niccolò a Cafaggio and also housed the Conservatory of Music and the ancient and celebrated Opificio delle Pietre Dure, or factory for the working of semi-precious stones.

The largest group of paintings still came

The hall on the first floor

Below:
the Sala del Colosso

Pages 104-105:
view of the Galleria della Tribuna as it appeared in the late 1960s

from the medieval period and the Renaissance, but contemporary works were gradually added to the collection, some of them bought by Grand Duke Leopoldo II. The most important development, however, and the one to which the Accademia owes its fame today, was the arrival of Michelangelo's *David*. The famous statue was removed from Piazza della Signoria for reasons of conservation and placed in the Gallery (1873), where a few years later a special room was built for it. Known as the "Tribuna," this was designed by the architect Emilio De Fabris, principal of the school at the time. Ever since then the Gallery has received an unbroken flow of visitors, most of them drawn solely by a desire to take a close look at Michelangelo's masterpiece. And in the eyes of the public, the splendor and perfection of the *David* have often overshadowed the museum's other treasures, such as the collection of fourteenth-century Tuscan pictures – one of the richest groups of paintings on a "gold ground" in the world – along with an extensive range of works from the sixteenth century and the Counter Reformation and an unusual collection of ancient Russian and Cretan icons.

Subsequent renovations and alterations have sought, over the years, to create a more rational arrangement of the works, and have also permitted the display of an interesting group of nineteenth-century plaster casts by Lorenzo Bartolini – an important sculptor and illustrious professor of the Academy – and Luigi Pampaloni, in a large room known as the Salone delle Toscane. On its walls hang some of the paintings that won competitions staged by the Academy, establishing a link between the present Gallery and its ancient origins.

Francesco Granacci
(Florence 1469 – 1543)
■ *Our Lady of the Assumption with Saints*
Sala del Colosso
panel, 301.5x217 cm
The majority of works in this room, known as the Sala del Colosso or "Room of the Colossus," because in the nineteenth century it housed a plaster copy of one of the two *Dioscuri* from Monte Cavallo (Rome), are large altarpieces from the early decades of the sixteenth century. They include this painting by Granacci, which has recently been restored and can therefore now be seen in its true colors. It was painted for the church of San Giorgio alla Costa in Florence, around 1520, and the imposing figures show the artistic influence of Michelangelo, with whom Granacci had a long and close friendship,

dating back to the time when they were both apprentices in Ghirlandaio's workshop. There are also references to other important contemporary painters such as Raphael, Fra Bartolomeo, and Mariotto Albertinelli.

Filippino Lippi (Prato 1457 – Florence 1504) and **Pietro Vannucci**, called **Perugino** (Città della Pieve 1445/50 – Fontignano, Perugia, 1523)
■ *Deposition*
Sala del Colosso
panel, 334x225 cm
This panel, like the complex polyptych to which it belonged, was commissioned from Filippino Lippi in 1503 for the altar of the church of Santissima Annunziata. On his death, just a few months later, the work was

entrusted to Perugino, and the painting now bears the predominant stamp of his style. Filippino's contribution, on the other hand, is chiefly visible in the upper part of the picture. In the complex interlacing of bodies, ribbons, and arms that represents the removal of Christ from the cross we find, in fact, the fanciful and flowing forms favored by Lippi, made still more evident by the contrast with the rigid geometry of the cross and ladders. In the lower section, filled with mourning figures, we can recognize the manner of Perugino: terse and composed, it is an expression of deep religious feelings. Some of the figures (St. John and the Magdalen) may even have been painted by the young Raphael.

Bartolomeo della Porta, called **Fra Bartolomeo** (Florence 1472 – 1517)
■ *The Prophets Job and Isaiah*
Sala del Colosso
panels, 169x108 cm (each)
These *Prophets*, like the *Deposition* by Perugino and Filippino Lippi, were painted for a chapel in the church of Santissima Annunziata. They formed the wings of an altarpiece representing the *Salvator Mundi*, now in the Palatine Gallery, commissioned by the Florentine merchant, Salvatore Billi.
The figures of the two prophets may have been painted in 1516, as was the central panel, but it is also possible that they date from slightly earlier and should therefore be connected with a journey the artist made to Rome. In fact the two prophets show evident links with Michelangelo's frescoes in the Sistine Chapel, sharing their monumentality and shimmering colors.

Andrea del Sarto (Florence 1486 – 1530)
■ *Christ in Pity*
Sala del Colosso
detached fresco, 182x113 cm
The fresco was originally located at the top of a staircase, in the novitiate of the convent of the Santissima Annunziata. In fact the figure of Christ is foreshortened, with a point of view set low down. This amplifies the monumental effect and gives emphasis to the powerful anatomy, represented with rapid and sure brushstrokes. Yet emotional intensity and a heartfelt piety prevail over the grandeur of the fresco in Christ's abandoned limbs, in his head bent under the weight of infinite suffering and in the pale and transparent colors that impart a simplicity to the scene.

Michelangelo Buonarroti
(Caprese, Arezzo, 1475 – Rome 1564)
■ *David*
Tribuna
marble, ht. 410 cm

In 1501, the Vestry Board of Florence
Cathedral commissioned Michelangelo to
carve a statue of David from an enormous
block of marble at which two other sculptors,
Agostino di Duccio (1462-63) and Antonio
Rossellino (1470), had already tried their
hand. The characteristics and dimensions of
the marble proved no obstacle to the young
Michelangelo. It took three years of constant
labor to complete his masterpiece, as Vasari
admiringly relates. His contemporaries
immediately grasped the value of the work
and the special commission of artists and
notable citizens appointed to choose a location
for the work decided on the City Hall,
emphasizing the civil significance of the
sculpture – interpreted as a symbol of freedom
– over the religious one.

Michelangelo himself had made profound
changes to the iconography of David, known
in Florence through other celebrated
sculptures by Donatello and Verrocchio (now
in the Museo del Bargello) that represented
him as a young adolescent with his feet shod
and head covered and Goliath's head at his
feet. Michelangelo chose, instead, to carve the
heroic figure of a young man, his perfect and
elegantly proportioned body inspired by the
harmony of ancient sculptures: naked and
without the head of Goliath, he is perhaps
depicted at the moment preceding the
combat. The statue conveys an unprecedented
sense of psychological concentration, where
the unease revealed by the tension of the
muscles is balanced by the intensity of the
resolute and confident gaze.

There are also innovative features in the
treatment of the material, which produces
highly effective results through the different
textures of the surface, smooth as a thin layer
of skin through which the throbbing nerves
can be seen in the body and hands, rough in
the leather of the sling, and stiff in the irregular
bark of the tree trunk behind David's leg.

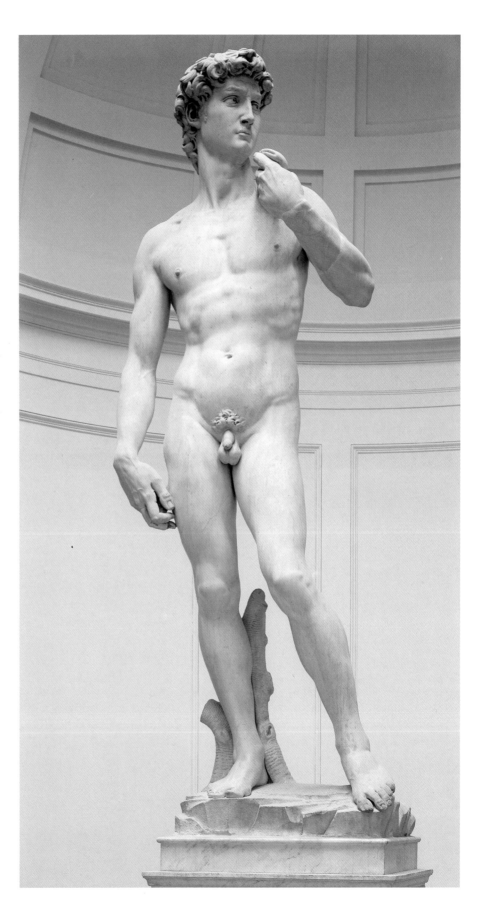

Michelangelo

■ *Prisoner* known as the *Awakening Slave*, marble, ht. 267 cm; *Prisoner* known as *Atlas,* marble, ht. 277 cm; *Prisoner* known as the *Young Slave*, marble, ht. 256 cm; *Prisoner* known as the *Bearded Slave*, marble, ht. 263 cm

Set along the walls of the gallery of the Tribuna, they appear, at first impact, to be put into the shade by the imposing beauty of the *David*. On closer examination, however, you are struck by the curious nature of these unfinished sculptures, which look as if they are making slow and laborious efforts to free themselves from the matter in which they are embedded. And in this contrast between still indeterminate material and parts that are already powerfully modeled, they offer the most effective examples of Michelangelo's *non-finito*, or technique of leaving works unfinished. Along with the two earlier *Slaves* in the Louvre and the statue of *Victory* in Palazzo Vecchio, the *Prisoners* in the Accademia (1530-34) were to have formed a grand sepulchral monument to Pope Julius II in St. Peter's, for which Michelangelo had received the commission as far back as 1505. The construction of this tomb proved an extremely difficult task, undergoing numerous modifications to the design and the original location and dragging on for over forty years. The end result only reflected a fraction of the grandeur of the initial design. These figures of "prisoners" were to have occupied the lower part of the monument. Recent interpretations have seen them as symbolizing the struggle of humanity to free itself from the bonds of sin, casting off the chains of matter that oppress it. This would also explain the author's deliberate use of the *non-finito* technique.

Unfortunately there was no room for them in the final version of the monument and they remained in Michelangelo's house in Florence. After his death, his nephew Leonardo gave them (1564) to Grand Duke Cosimo I, who set them up in the Grotto of Buontalenti in the Boboli Gardens. They were transferred from there to the Accademia at the beginning of the twentieth century.

Michelangelo

■ *Saint Matthew*
Galleria
marble, ht. 271 cm

Like the *Prisoners*, with which it shares the space along the walls of the gallery, the *Saint Matthew* was left in an unfinished state. Its origin is different, however, stemming from a commission (1503) from the Consuls of the Arte della Lana, or Wool Guild, who wanted to adorn the chapels of the chancel of Santa Maria del Fiore with a series of twelve apostles, carved out of Carrara marble. The *Saint Matthew* was the first to be made, between 1505 and 1506, but then the project was abandoned because of the artist's departure, when he was summoned to Rome by Julius II to fresco the Sistine Chapel. The one sculpture to have been carved remained for a long time in the courtyard of the Cathedral Vestry, from where it was removed in 1834 and taken to the Accademia. The same dramatic tension that permeates the *Prisoners* can also be seen in the *Saint Matthew*, but with a more evident sense of suffering, rendered tangible by the marked torsion of the body, from which the left leg sticks out forcefully. The rest of the figure remains embedded in the material, as if it were painfully restrained, an impression that Michelangelo conveys with great technical skill.

Michelangelo

■ *Palestrina Pietà*
Galleria
marble, ht. 253 cm

The sculpture comes from the Barberini Chapel in the church of Santa Rosalia at Palestrina (Rome), from which it takes its name.

There is no mention of the work in the records, and doubts have been raised as to whether it is really the work of Michelangelo. In fact it would have been uncharacteristic of Michelangelo to choose to work a piece of marble taken from an ancient building, as is shown by the traces of a decoration of acanthus leaves and patterned moldings still visible on the back. In addition, the flat and elongated shape of the piece of marble would have forced the artist to lay out his composition along parallel lines, excluding the three-dimensional effect typical of that phase in his production. Finally, further doubts are raised by the obvious lack of proportions in the figures, which show signs of clumsiness and error. These can only be explained by assuming the sculpture to be the work of an artist in Michelangelo's circle who, while familiar with the master's stylistic canons, was not capable of matching his powerful synthesis of expressiveness and imagination.

Alessio Baldovinetti
(Florence 1425 – 1499)
The Holy Trinity between Saints Benedict and John Gualberto
Sale fiorentine
panel, 238x284 cm
This work is a significant example of Florentine painting in the fifteenth century, which is amply documented in three rooms on the ground floor, known as the "Florentine Rooms." The large picture adorned the high altar of Santa Trinita, for which it was commissioned in 1470 by the patrons of the church, the Gianfigliazzi family. Only a year earlier they had had Baldovinetti fresco the entire main chapel with scenes from the Old Testament. All that remains of this decoration today are the evangelists on the ceiling and this panel in the Accademia. Unfortunately its original coloring has been destroyed by a clumsy attempt at restoration. Yet it is still recognizable as a picture of quality, in which the space, in the absence of any reference to a landscape, is structured by means of the cunning arrangement of the figures. The sweeping orchestration of the composition is reminiscent of similarly crowded works by Fra Angelico, with whom Baldovinetti collaborated.

Giovanni di Ser Giovanni,
called **Scheggia** (San Giovanni Valdarno 1406 – Florence 1486)
■ *Wedding Procession* (*Adimari Chest*)
Sale fiorentine
panel, 63x280 cm
Recently, thanks to the studies of Luciano

Bellosi, it has been possible to give a name to the author of this panel: Giovanni di Ser Giovanni, called Scheggia, the younger brother of Masaccio. Even the date, previously thought to be 1420 because this was the year of the marriage between Boccaccio Adimari and Lisa Ricasoli – which the panel was traditionally believed to represent – has been shifted to a significantly later time (1440-50), on the basis of stylistic considerations. In addition, it has been recognized that the panel does not come from a wedding chest, but from a *spalliera*, a fifteenth-century piece of furniture that was used in aristocratic homes

to protect the walls of rooms from the cold. The work has been the subject of careful study because it can tell us a great deal about the customs of the time, offering delightful glimpses of city life – set against the backdrop of the unmistakable profile of the Baptistery – and a rich sample of clothing and costumes that attest to the high level of quality attained by Florentine weavers during the Renaissance period.

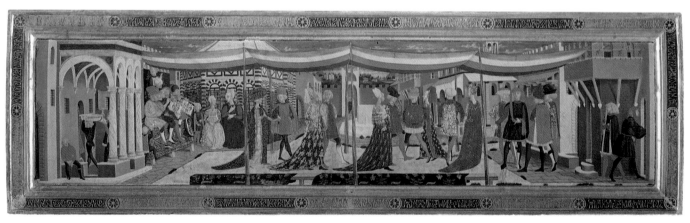

Paolo di Dono, called **Paolo Uccello**
(Pratovecchio, Arezzo, 1397 – Florence 1475)
■ *Thebaid*
Sale fiorentine
canvas, 81x111 cm
The fanciful character of this representation of monastic life has led, notwithstanding difficulties of attribution and disagreement among critics, to the small canvas being assigned to Paolo Uccello, the artist most committed, in the mid fifteenth century, to experimentation with perspective as well as a painter of unusual subjects.
The work comes from the Vallombrosian monastery of San Giorgio alla Costa, but it seems likely that it was originally in a Franciscan monastery. In fact several preaching saints can be identified in the composite scene: Francis, Bernard, and Benedict. Owing to apparent affinities with works painted by the artist in the 1470s, distinguished by a circumstantial and lively sense of anecdote – particularly evident in the *Hunt in the Forest* in Oxford – some critics have assigned the picture to that period.

Alessandro Filipepi, called **Botticelli**
(Florence 1445 – 1510)
■ *Madonna and Child, the Young Saint John, and Two Angels*
Sale fiorentine
panel, 85x64 cm
This early work by Botticelli can be dated to around 1470, as suggested by the still tense character of the style, which does not yet have the fluidity of line and gentle caressing of forms typical of the artist's mature work.

Even the colors have colder tones, and the heads of children that form an arch around the beautiful head of the Madonna with its rapt expression, while of high quality, still bear the mark of his first teacher, Filippo Lippi. The carefully drawn outlines and the plasticity of the figures, on the other hand, seem to be derived directly from Verrocchio, in whose workshop Botticelli was employed at the time. The work comes from the hospital of Santa Maria Nuova in Florence.

Attributed to **Sandro Botticelli**
■ *Madonna del Mare*
Sale fiorentine
panel, 40x28 cm
In comparison with the other picture by Botticelli, this *Madonna* shows signs of an evolution toward a softer and more fluid line. However, the attribution to the painter is not unanimous and recently the picture has been assigned to Filippino Lippi. It is not easy to distinguish the styles of the two artists, who were both pupils of Filippino's father. In any case the result is of high quality, showing great delicacy in the atmospheric seascape in the background from which the picture takes its name (*Madonna of the Sea*), as well as in the features of the two figures and the graceful manner in which the Madonna clasps the Child.

Lorenzo di Credi (Florence ca. 1460 – 1537)
■ *Jesus adored by the Virgin, Saint Joseph, and Two Angels*
Sale fiorentine
panel, 138x144 cm
This painting, in which a serene and devout sense of piety holds sway, seems to have been conceived under the influence of the strict teachings of Savonarola, of whom Lorenzo di Credi was an open follower. However, it is also possible to detect the influence of contemporary great Florentine painting, with which he had come into contact in Verrocchio's workshop, where the young Leonardo had also served his apprenticeship, while the realistic attention to the fabrics, hair, and landscape in the distance are signs of a general interest in Flemish art. The refined and intellectual note of the half-ruined architecture suggests that it dates from the last decade of the fifteenth century, and has a famous precedent in Botticelli's *Adoration of the Magi*, now in the Uffizi.

Raffaello de' Carli, called **Raffaellino del Garbo** (Florence 1466 – 1525)
■ *Resurrection of Christ*
Sale fiorentine
panel, 177x187 cm

This work, whose gaudy colors have been revealed by restoration, displays obvious references to the style of Filippino Lippi, from whom the artist received his training, in the animated composition and fluttering drapery. There are also affinities with Umbrian painting, well-known to and much appreciated by the artist, which seems to have influenced the definition of the landscape. The picture is considered one of Raffaellino's most successful works and the majority of critics date it to around 1505, in view of the fact that some of the soldiers – in particular the one crushed by the lid of the sarcophagus – appear to be a direct citation of the cartoon for the *Battle of Cascina*, made by Leonardo in 1504. The fine head of the soldier sleeping behind the sarcophagus is identified by Vasari as a portrait of Niccolò Capponi, a member of the family who raised and protected the artist.

Giuliano Bugiardini
(Florence 1475 – 1554)
■ *Madonna and Child with the Young Saint John*
Lateral arms of the Tribuna
panel, 117x88 cm
In this picture, in which the painter

demonstrates the composite nature of his cultural background, the most pertinent artistic reference appears to be to Raphael's *Esterházy Madonna* (ca. 1508), of which the composition, softness, and intimacy of the scene is a reflection. The small scroll near the bottom edge of the painting is inscribed with the author's name and the date of the picture, which entered the Gallery as an acquisition.

Master of the Magdalen

(Florence, second half of 13th cent.)
■ *Penitent Magdalen and Eight Scenes from Her Life*
Sale bizantine
panel, 164x76 cm

This is one of the most significant paintings in the Sale bizantine, or Byzantine Rooms, named after a group of works that was generically assigned to that school in the past. We do not know much about the anonymous artist who must have painted it around 1280, but scholars have grouped under his name a series of pictures that may have come out of his active workshop. This *Magdalen* shows certain affinities with the mosaics in Florence Baptistery and reveals a liveliness in the depiction of features and in narrative that marks the beginning of a direct relationship with the observer.

Jacopo Carrucci, called Pontormo

(Pontorme, Empoli, 1495 – Florence 1556)
■ *Venus and Cupid*
Lateral arms of the Tribuna
panel, 127x191 cm

This work constitutes an interesting testimony to the artistic ties between Michelangelo and Pontormo, with the former providing the preparatory drawing (1533) and the latter turning it into a painting. This cooperation had already produced a *Noli me tangere* now in Casa Buonarroti. The most obvious trace of Michelangelo's composition remains in the powerful nude in the foreground, freely inspired by the frescoes in the Sistine Chapel, while the symbolic references and the landscape in the background bear the more personal mark of Pontormo. The picture was painted for the nuptial chamber of Bartolomeo Bettini and the cultured references and symbols should be seen in relation to that setting, which had already been decorated with lunettes by Bronzino.

is an example of the effort to develop a simpler and truer kind of art, based on precepts of clarity of form in keeping with the directions issued by the Church in the Counter Reformation, and very different from the intellectualistic abstractions of Mannerist painting. A prominent figure in the current of artists influenced by the Counter Reformation, Santi di Tito painted numerous religious compositions with a markedly didactic character.

Santi di Tito

(Sansepolcro 1536 – Florence 1603)
■ *Christ's Entry into Jerusalem*
Lateral arms of the Tribuna
panel, 350x230 cm

The picture was painted for the church of Monteoliveto, near Florence, in the 1570s. It

with forty-seven tondi illustrating the main episodes of his life.

The careful and painstaking choreography of the panel is a typical demonstration of Pacino's qualities as a skilled and patient illuminator.

Giovanni da Milano (Caversaccio, Como, documented from 1346 to 1369)
■ *Christ in Pity*
Sale bizantine
panel, 122x58 cm
The small cuspidate panel, as the inscription tells us, is the work (1365) of Giovanni da Milano, an important artist of the second half of the fourteenth century. He was able to reconcile the linear grace of his northern training with a study of Giotto's handling of volumes. The picture comes from the monastery of San Girolamo sulla Costa and was painted during one of the most prolific periods of his career, at a time when he was also working on the frescoes in the Rinuccini Chapel in Santa Croce.

Pacino di Bonaguida
(Florence, documented from 1303 to 1330)
■ *Tree of Life*
Sale bizantine
panel, 248x151 cm
This immense tree of life, painted by Pacino di Bonaguida between 1305 and 1310, takes its inspiration from the *Lignum vitae* that St. Bonaventure wrote in 1274. Some of the

scrolls carry lengthy passages from this text, along with others drawn from the Bible, including *Revelation* and the *Song of Songs*, in a sort of curious "Bible of the poor" (*Biblia pauperum*) entrusted with the task of conveying messages through visual representation.

At the center of the picture is set Christ on the cross, from which spread out twelve branches

Piero di Giovanni, called **Lorenzo Monaco** (Siena? ca. 1370 – Florence 1423/24)

■ *Agony in the Garden*
Rooms on the second floor
panel, 222x109 cm

The work comes from the monastery of Santa Maria degli Angeli, where Lorenzo Monaco lived after taking vows as a Camaldolensian monk. Here he learned the art of illumination, of which he became a refined exponent, and his skill in drawing and coloring is also apparent in his panel paintings. The Gallery contains an exceptional number of these pictures. This *Agony* can be assigned to the early part of his career.

Andrea di Cione, called **Orcagna**
(Florence, documented from 1343 to 1368)

■ *Pentecost*
Rooms on the second floor
panel, 195x287 cm
The hieratic and somewhat archaic frontality of this altarpiece painted for the church of Santi Apostoli should not mislead us about the date of its execution, which must have been somewhere between the end of the 1360s and the beginning of the following decade.
The painting displays, in contrast, a great deal of inventiveness in the disposition of the twelve apostles within a restricted space, in a

circular arrangement that creates a sense of depth. It is possible to recognize the decisive brushwork of this versatile artist, who made the celebrated tabernacle in Orsanmichele, although it would not be out of place to suggest a collaboration with Spinello Aretino.

Bernardo Daddi
(Florence, late 13th cent. – 1348)

■ *Painted Cross*
Sale bizantine
panel, 350x275 cm
The cross has recently been restored, with results that confirm the great ability of the artist, who has long suffered from the negative view of him held by Roberto Longhi. In this work too, Daddi showed that he had assimilated the lesson of Giotto, but developed it in terms of a vertical and sinuous linearity, exemplified by the figures of the Virgin and St. John, curiously represented full length instead of half. Note the animated scenes in the panels set at the ends of the arms, representing scenes from the Passion.

father, Bicci di Lorenzo, he maintained solid ties with this style, favoring compositions of a vertical character, as is apparent in this *Annunciation*. The picture is mentioned in the book of records drawn up by the artist – an important source of information about his workshop's activity – and was painted in 1464 for the Florentine monastery of the Campora.

Giovanni del Biondo
(Florence, documented from 1356 to 1399)
■ *Annunciation*
Rooms on the second floor
panel, 406x377 cm
This is one of the richest and most elaborate works in the section of the Gallery devoted to the fourteenth century. Painted by Giovanni del Biondo with the help of assistants, it adorned the altar of the Cavalcanti Chapel in the church of Santa Maria Novella, and must have been painted around 1380. The polyptych is a significant example of the size and complexity that altarpieces had attained by this time. They were works requiring great craftsmanship but which tended to make use of tried and tested pictorial styles.

Neri di Bicci (Florence, 1419 – 1492)
■ *Annunciation*
Rooms on the second floor
panel, 152x154 cm
Trained in the late Gothic workshop of his

Agnolo Gaddi
(Florence, documented from 1369 to 1396)
■ *Madonna dell'Umiltà*
Rooms on the second floor
panel, 118x58 cm
This fine picture representing the "Madonna of Humility" was painted toward the end of the artist's career. It comes from the convent of Santa Verdiana and its intimate tone suggests that it was intended for private devotion. The forms of the Madonna and Child are influenced by Giotto's style, with which the painter was familiar through his father Taddeo, Giotto's most faithful collaborator, but the iconography chosen and the many carefully studied details show that it was still an expression of late Gothic culture.

MUSEO DI SAN MARCO

As soon as you enter the monastery of San Marco, now the museum *par excellence* of Fra Angelico but also housing an important collection of sixteenth- and seventeenth-century devotional painting, you will realize "that this place was once a perfect 'machine' for living, studying, and praying, a 'city of God' set in the tumultuous city of men." In fact, crossing the threshold and leaving behind the chaotic bustle of the square, you enter the peace and quiet of one of the complex's two great cloisters, the one dedicated to St. Antonino, Dominican prior of the monastery and then archbishop of Florence in the middle of the fifteenth century. The story of his life is illustrated on the walls of the cloister by frescoes that have faded with the passing of time but that still constitute an important repertory of seventeenth-century painting (Bernardino Poccetti, Fabrizio Boschi, Matteo Rosselli, etc.). From this open space, which bears the stamp of Michelozzo's architectural rigor, you enter the rooms that once measured the rhythm of the monks' life and are now used as exhibition spaces. The visitor will have an opportunity to reflect on the modern functionality that Michelozzo, Cosimo the Elder's favorite architect, impressed on the

Michelozzo's Library

Left:
the Cloister of Saint
Antonino

Below:
view of one of the
corridors leading to the
dormitories

Pages 120-121:
Fra Angelico
San Marco Altarpiece;
predella: Burial of
Cosmas and Damian
with their Brothers
Pilgrims' Hospice

monastery in the work that he carried out between 1436 and 1446, restructuring what had previously been the seat of the Sylvestrine monks. Without question, the first stop to be made on any visit is the former pilgrims' hospice, the room that, used as a refuge, was logically placed close to the monastery's entrance. Today it houses the collection of Fra Angelico's panel paintings, brought here from churches and monasteries in Florence and its immediate surroundings. The next stages on the tour of the museum are the former chapterhouse – where the monks used to meet to discuss problems linked to community life – occupied by Fra Angelico's great *Crucifixion*; the two refectories, the smaller frescoed by Ghirlandaio, the larger by Sogliani; the guest's quarters; and the service rooms that have been turned into exhibition spaces. On the upper floor are located three long corridors, providing access to the small cells of the monks frescoed by Fra Angelico and his collaborators, and the large library, Michelozzo's architectural masterpiece and the pride of the monastery. It was here that Cosimo housed ancient Italian, Latin, and Greek codices that used to belong to a scholar named Niccolò Niccoli, and it was the first place that he wanted to be open to the public. Today it contains illuminated choir books, some of them of great value, which for reasons of conservation are dis-

played in rotation. This is perhaps the part of the building that has the most monastic atmosphere, pervaded by a sense of both humanity and spirituality, in which the severity of the architecture is in perfect harmony with the pictorial decoration. Making the museum complex the most eloquent example in Florence of the relationship between humanity, art, and the religious spirit that was typical of the Renaissance.

Ever since it was founded, in 1869, the museum has set out to make the most of all these artistic testimonies hitherto closed to the public, and at the same time to document the history of which it had been the setting for long centuries.

The fact is that prominent figures in the city's life have passed much of their existence within these walls, in a fascinating blend of wider history and the private dimension. Thus it is possible to visit the cells occupied by the sainted bishop Antonino and by Girolamo Savonarola, the Ferrarese preacher famous for his "bonfire of vanities," who lived here as prior of the monastery and who was arrested here in 1498, before being burned at the stake as a heretic and rabble-rouser. Even Cosimo the Elder had a cell set aside for him where he could go to seek solace in meditation, far from the intrigues of politics, and in more recent times another outstanding personality in the city's political and spiritual life, Giorgio La Pira, the "sainted" mayor famous all over the world for his work on behalf of peace, found a refuge and home within these walls, demonstrating yet again just how strong is the link between San Marco and the city.

Guido di Pietro, called **Fra Angelico**
(Vicchio ca. 1395 – Rome 1455) and **Pietro
di Giovanni**, called **Lorenzo Monaco**
(Siena? ca. 1370 – Florence 1423/24)

■ *Deposition*
Pilgrims' Hospice
panel, 185x176 cm
A work from Fra Angelico's artistic maturity
and, perhaps, his masterpiece. It can be seen
in the former pilgrim's hospice along with a
rich selection of the artist's panel paintings. It
was commissioned from Lorenzo Monaco by

Palla Strozzi for the sacristy and family chapel
in the church of Santa Trinita, but at the time
of his death the painter had completed only
the cusps and some parts of the predella, now
in the Accademia. By the beginning of the
1430s Fra Angelico had finished it, brilliantly
resolving the problem of setting such a vast
composition within a tripartite, typically
Gothic framework. The devotional timbre of
the painting, which pivots around the body of
Christ at the center of the picture, dissolves in
the background into two beautiful landscapes,

constructed on the basis of a skillful
interpretation of Renaissance perspective. In
these backdrops and in the limpid modeling
of the figures, Fra Angelico blends the results
of Masaccio's innovations with his own highly
personal figurative vocabulary.

Fra Angelico

■ *Last Judgment*
Pilgrims' Hospice
panel, 105x210 cm
The unusual shape of this painting, which
dates from the time of the *Deposition* in Santa
Trinita (1431), has led to the conclusion that
it formed the upper section of the back of the

chorister's bench in the church of Santa Maria
degli Angeli, now destroyed.
The observer's eye cannot avoid being drawn
by the virtuoso perspective of the row of
uncovered tombs, at the center, which
stretches into the distance and divides the
space of the elect from that of the damned, in
a break with the traditional medieval

iconography in which they are represented on
separate levels. In the crowd of figures that fills
the painting there are many references to
Dante, who must also have been the figurative
source for Fra Angelico's painting of *Hell* on
the walls of the Camposanto in Pisa. In the
scenery of the mountain and the garden of
delights, where the painter also displays his
most exquisite decorative style, Fra Angelico
attempts a realistic representation of space.

Fra Angelico

■ *Naming of the Baptist*
Pilgrims' Hospice
panel, 26x24 cm
This small panel must have been painted by
1435, as this is the date of a copy by the artist
Andrea di Giusto, now in the Museo Civico of
Prato. Scholars are in agreement that it was
originally part of a dismembered polyptych.
Another fragment, similar in size and style, is
in the Kimbell Art Museum at Fort Worth
(Texas).
The scene, with its intense and lively dialogue
between the figures, is set in a well-defined
and limpid space, framed by the architecture
of Michelozzo.

Fra Angelico
- *Linaioli Triptych*
Pilgrims' Hospice
panel, 292x176 cm (closed)

Fra Angelico painted this triptych, which was
his first public commission and one of his
most imposing works, for the Guild of Linen
Drapers, Ragmen, and Tailors in 1433. So the
work represents a moment of transition
between his early work and the period of his
artistic maturity. It was a time when he must
have come under the influence of Ghiberti, the
famous sculptor who designed the triptych's
marble frame, carved by two of his apprentices,
Jacopo di Bartolomeo da Settignano and Simone
di Nanni da Fiesole. Ghiberti's influence is
most evident in the two evangelists, Mark and
Peter, portrayed on the outside of the leaves,
who resemble the apostles that the sculptor
had carved in marble for Orsanmichele.

Fra Angelico
- *Bosco ai Frati Altarpiece*
Pilgrims' Hospice
panel, 174x174 cm; 26x174 cm (predella)

This altarpiece has a monumental appearance,
both in its figures and in the "pre-
Bramantesque" architectural backdrop,
probably inspired by the painter's contacts
with Michelozzo and his visits to Rome. It
was ordered by Cosimo de' Medici for the
monastery of San Bonaventura al Bosco, in
Mugello. He must have received the
commission around 1438, at the time when
Michelozzo was working on the restructuring
of the monastery, but Fra Angelico painted
the picture some time afterward, judging by
its classical sumptuousness. Another reason
for assigning it a later date is the presence, in
the predella, of St. Bernardino, who was not
canonized until 1450.

Fra Angelico
- *Lamentation over the Dead Christ*
Pilgrims' Hospice
panel, 105x164 cm

The work comes from an oratory close to the
Arno. This explains the damage visible in the
lower part of the panel, caused by the frequent
flooding to which the river was subject. The
date 1441 is engraved on the border of the
Madonna's mantle and is probably the year it
was painted, although the documents tell us
that it was commissioned by the Dominican
friar Sebastiano Benintendenti in 1436. He
wanted the picture to include his ancestor the
Blessed Villana delle Botti, along with St.
Catherine of Alexandria, as he was in charge

of celebrations in her honor. As in fourteenth-century pictures of the same subject, the composition is crowded with saints and does not adhere to fifteenth-century precepts of order and balance. Instead, all the drama of the event is concentrated in the horizontal undulating rhythm. In the background, however, the light playing over the walled city of Jerusalem, depicted in rigorous perspective, seems to overlay the agitated sense of grief with an atmosphere of suspended hope.

Fra Angelico and **Alessio Baldovinetti** (Florence 1425 – 1499)

■ *Doors of the Silver Cabinet*
Pilgrims' Hospice
panels, 123x123; 123x160; 123x160 cm

The panels were originally the doors of the cabinet used to store votive offerings in the oratory of the Santissima Annunziata. It is said that Piero de' Medici commissioned them from Fra Angelico in 1448, but it is more likely that the work was carried out a few years later, since the oratory itself was not created until 1453. In that same year Fra Angelico was summoned to Rome to paint the frescoes in the Vatican and they were finished by his collaborators, including Baldovinetti. The cabinet was moved to a different location in the seventeenth century and broken up the following century. Although the overall iconographic layout and the execution of the first nine panels can be ascribed to Fra Angelico, many other artists contributed to this work from his maturity. The cycle depicts thirty-five episodes from the *Life of Christ*, and in each scene great attention is paid to the architectural settings and to a realistic representation of space.

Fra Angelico

▪ *Saint Dominic in Adoration of the Crucifix*
Cloister of Sant'Antonino
fresco, 340x206 cm

This large fresco, part of the great cycle of decorations that extends right through the monastery, is located in one of its "communal" spaces, the cloister of Sant'Antonino, situated near the door leading into the adjoining church. As in all the more conspicuous frescoes in the monastery, the painter made abundant use of azurite, the costly pigment that, like gold, was reserved for works of great importance. The imposing crucifix, adored by the guardian saint of the monastery, became a model for the others scattered around the dormitory (there are eighteen of them in the cells) and was intended to convey, through the expression of the saint and the accentuation of Christ's anatomy, a constant spiritual message to the friars of San Marco.

Fra Angelico

▪ *Crucifixion with Saints*
Chapterhouse
fresco, 550x950 cm

The fresco (1442) occupies the rear wall of the former chapterhouse and the importance of the location – the place where the friars held their meetings – justifies the monumental

tone of the picture, in which the barren backdrop, almost devoid of elements of scenery, helps to increase the tragic atmosphere of the event. Today, however, the stretch of sky that used to frame the three crosses can no longer be appreciated in its original glory, as the loss of the azurite has allowed the gray and red priming of the ground to show through.

On the left are depicted the saints linked to Florence and its grand dukes, Cosmas and Damian, Mark, Lawrence, and John the Baptist, accompanied by an almost scenographic crowd of sacred figures. Below the fresco runs a molding of medallions that enclose, in addition to St. Dominic, half-length portraits of the most illustrious friars of the Dominican order.

Giovanni Antonio Sogliani
(Florence 1492 – 1544)
■ *Saint Dominic's Miraculous Supper*
Large Refectory
fresco, 500x792 cm

This large fresco is painted on the rear wall of the former refectory, which now houses a significant collection of panel paintings, dating from the sixteenth-seventeenth century, influenced by Fra Bartolomeo's devotional painting. In fact, in his *Miraculous Supper*, signed and dated 1536, Sogliani combines a clarity of composition derived from Fra Bartolomeo with the sixteenth-century legacy of Andrea del Sarto's delicately shaded coloring. We do not know how much credibility to attach to the claim made in the old sources that there used to be a fresco of a *Crucifixion* by Fra Angelico on the same wall. What is certain is that Sogliani managed to blend the theme of the *Crucifixion*, frequent

in fourteenth-century iconography, with that of the *Last Supper*, typical of the new figurative language of the Renaissance. The depiction of an episode from the life of St. Dominic was, in any case, closely linked to the Dominicans of San Marco, who undoubtedly provided the painter with iconographic instructions.

Fra Bartolomeo
■ *Saint Mary Magdalene*
Fra Bartolomeo Room
fresco on tile, 47x35 cm
This curious painting on a tile should have
inserted, along with several others, in the wall
of the Dominican monastery of the
Maddalena at Caldine, near Fiesole, where Fra
Bartolomeo died. It is on show along with
other works by the friar painter, who lived and
worked in San Marco, in the room dedicated
to him, the monastery's former kitchen which
has been converted into an exhibition space.
The fresco, with its diffuse and delicate
coloring, is an excellent example of Fra
Bartolomeo's religious painting.

Bartolomeo della Porta, called **Fra
Bartolomeo** (Florence 1472 – 1517)
■ *Madonna and Child with Saint Ann
and other Saints*
Fra Bartolomeo Room
panel, 444x305 cm
The painting was commissioned (1510) by
Piero Soderini, Gonfalonier of the Republic,
for a prestigious location, the new Council
Chamber in Palazzo Vecchio. In fact the
picture, along with works by Leonardo and
Michelangelo, was intended to celebrate the
free and democratic Florence that had been
created by the overthrow of the Medici family.
Even the theme chosen, a discussion of the
Immaculate Conception, would have been
well-suited to a room where lively debates
were going to take place. However, the work
was never finished, since the Medici returned
in 1513, when it was still at the preparatory
stage, and dissolved the Grand Council.

Attributed to **Alessio Baldovinetti**
■ *Saint Anthony in Adoration of the
Crucifix*
Baldovinetti Room
canvas, 276x147 cm
This large canvas, originally a processional
banner, is displayed in the room devoted to
Baldovinetti and other artists who were
influenced by Fra Angelico's style.
The documents attribute this *Crucifix* to the
Pollaiolo brothers, but its style is closer to that
of Baldovinetti in the 1470s. The backdrop of
cypresses attempts to use lines of perspective

in the manner of Fra Angelico – with whom
Baldovinetti collaborated on the panels for the
reliquary cabinet in the church of Santissima
Annunziata – but Christ's chest and the
drapery of the clothes show a greater interest
in drawing that reveals the painter's
sympathies for Andrea del Castagno and, of
course, Antonio and Piero del Pollaiolo.

Fra Angelico

■ *Annunciation*

Dormitories

fresco, 230x297 cm

When we think of Fra Angelico this is perhaps
the work that first comes to mind, a perfect
example of the innovations in painting that
took place in the fifteenth century, allowing it
to put across powerful messages. In addition
the fresco is located in a conspicuous position,
greeting visitors today at the end of the
staircase leading to the upper floor, just as it
used to be the first thing the monks saw on
entering their dormitories.

The restoration of the fresco has given the
setting, a Michelozzian arcade inspired by the
monastery's architecture, back its elegant
classical appearance, rendered so suggestive by
its close correspondence to the real
architecture. The Madonna and the angel
keep faith with the painter's inclination toward
decorativeness, as is evident from the wings
and the curly hair of the figures' heads, but
their anatomical forms are also clearly-defined
in space. The fresco was probably begun
before his stay in Rome in the 1440s, and
finished a decade later.

Fra Angelico
- *Noli me tangere*
Dormitories, cell 1
fresco, 166x125 cm

Each of the small cells in the dormitories contains a lunette frescoed with a scene from the life of Christ, arranged without any precise chronological order but designed to serve as aids to the concentration and meditation of the monks. The undertaking was carried out under the supervision of Fra Angelico, who naturally made use of assistants, and was largely executed between 1438 and 1445. The scene illustrated here is located in the first cell and is characterized by its lively colors, employed in virtuoso fashion in the natural setting as well as in the figure of Christ dressed as a gardener.

Fra Angelico
- *Transfiguration*
Dormitories, cell 6
fresco, 181x152 cm

The figure of Christ is represented in the attitude of an imposing cross. The disciples, set around him in a ring, convey an impression of excited wonder and veneration, dazzled by the light of the Resurrection that reflects off the clothing. Among the saints, we find the inevitable figure of St. Dominic, rapt in deep meditation.

Fra Angelico
- *Annunciation*
Dormitories, cell 3
fresco, 176x148 cm

This *Annunciation* represents the same subject as the famous fresco at the entrance to the dormitories, but reflects its different and more intimate purpose. So we should not be surprised at the deliberate simplification of the architectural setting for the figures: the Madonna, here painted without her customary blue mantle that would have required the use of costly azurite, the angel, and St. Peter the Martyr making an invitation to prayer.

Fra Angelico

■ *Christ Mocked, the Virgin, and Saint Dominic*

Dormitories, cell 7

fresco, 187x151 cm

The scene is set against an almost abstract background that brings out the sculptural form of the figures. Christ is placed at the center, with the symbols of martyrdom : a guard spitting as a sign of contempt, the hands beating him, and a hand holding the rod that strikes him.

Fra Angelico

■ *Saint Dominic in Glory*

Library

painted parchment, Missal 558

This is just one example of the precious illuminations to be found in the codices and missals on display in rotation in the harmonious library designed by Michelozzo. It testifies to a less well-known aspect of Fra Angelico's activity, who presumably tried his hand at illumination as well in his youth.

Fra Angelico and **Benozzo di Lese**, called **Benozzo Gozzoli**

(Florence 1420 – Pistoia 1497)

■ *Adoration of the Magi*

Dormitories, cell 39

fresco, 175x357 cm

The lunette with the *Adoration* is located in one of the two communicating cells that Cosimo the Elder kept in the monastery for his moments of private meditation. While the design of the composition, of which the niche with *Christ in Pity* also forms part, is attributed to Fra Angelico, the painting seems to have been executed by Benozzo Gozzoli, who was one of the master's most active

collaborators in this undertaking. An elegant and exotic atmosphere holds sway, and this may have been prompted by the Council of Florence in 1439 reaffirming the union of Constantinople and Rome.

Anonymous Florentine artist

(late 15th – early 16th century)
■ *Piazza della Signoria with the Martyrdom of Savonarola*
Dormitories, Savonarola's cells
panel, 100x115 cm
This view of the city is of great documentary importance, since it not only records a significant event in civil and religious life, but also shows us what Florence looked like in the fifteenth century. In fact the city is clearly recognizable through some of its symbolic monuments. The picture now forms part of the decoration of the rooms that were once occupied by Savonarola.

Fra Bartolomeo

■ *Portrait of Fra Girolamo Savonarola*
Dormitories, Savonarola's cells
panel, 53x37 cm
As prior of the monastery of San Marco, Savonarola was entitled to three rooms: a cell, a study, and a chapel, which he kept until the year (1498) he was condemned to be burned as a heretic. Today these rooms house objects and relics of the Dominican preacher along with portraits of him painted by Fra Bartolomeo, who was a devoted follower of Savonarola. This portrait, in particular, was appreciated by Vasari, who recognized in it the temperament of Savonarola, as well as the artist's determination to reduce environmental and descriptive annotations to the essential.

Domenico Bigordi, called **Ghirlandaio**
(Florence 1449 – 1494)

■ *Last Supper*
Small Refectory
fresco, 420x780 cm

This large fresco by Ghirlandaio occupies the rear wall of the small refectory on the ground floor (near the staircase leading to the dormitories), formerly used by guests. It represents a subject familiar to the painter, who over a brief span of time (ca. 1476-1480) completed another three versions of it.

The best-known of these is the one in the former refectory of the church of Ognissanti. The unusually square room, in comparison with the normally elongated shape of refectories, must have prompted the artist to give his painting a greater illusion of depth, through the representation of the table in perspective. And for the same reason Ghirlandaio took great care over the airy landscape in the background, filled with trees and birds. The scene contains many symbolic elements: from the peacocks alluding to the

Resurrection to the cat, a diabolic animal situated close to Judah, and from the cypresses, a symbol of death, to the palms representing martyrdom.

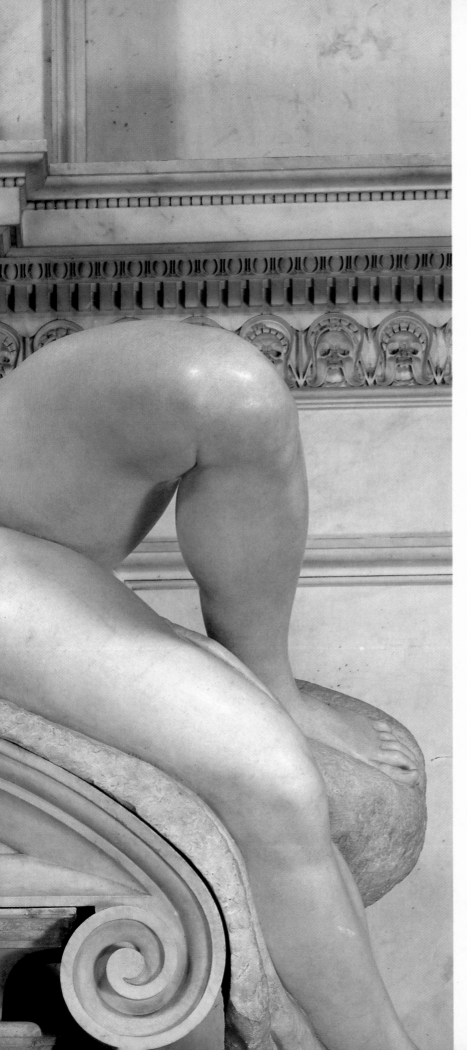

THE MEDICI CHAPELS

The monumental complex of the Medici Chapels, annexed to the church of San Lorenzo, consists of a crypt in which the members of the Medici family are buried, the Chapel of the Princes, a sumptuous expression of their power, and the so-called New Sacristy, on which Michelangelo worked as architect and sculptor. In fact San Lorenzo had been the Medici family church from the outset, as they had financed much of its construction. From the outside, the hemispherical vault over the perfectly cubical volume of the New Sacristy can be seen above the right arm of the transept. The cupola is topped by an elegant marble lantern, adorned with leonine forms in gilded copper alluding to the name of Leo X, the Medici pope who commenced construction of this building in 1520 in memory of his father Lorenzo the Magnificent. In contrast with the sobriety of Michelangelo's building, the external architecture of the Chapel of the Princes and the crypt is surprisingly grandiose and opulent in appearance. The original design by Don Giovanni de' Medici, Cosimo I's illegitimate son and winner of the competition staged in 1602, was revised by Bernardo Buontalenti. The work was supervised, from 1604 to 1649, by Matteo

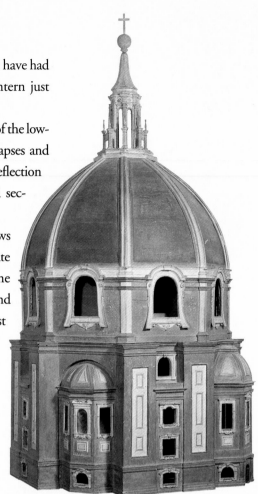

the crypt) was even supposed to have had ribs of white marble and a lantern just like the cathedral's on top.

Even the animated subdivision of the lower part of the chapel, with its apses and projecting blocks is clearly a reflection of the equally complex apsidal section of Santa Maria del Fiore.

The large and bizarre windows with curved lintels that decorate the walls underneath the dome were designed by Ferdinando and Giuseppe Ruggeri at the behest of Electress Palatine Anna Ludovica de' Medici.

Nigetti. The style of the architecture deliberately echoes that of the nearby cathedral of Santa Maria del Fiore, especially in the dome of identical coloring that, in the project of completion presented by Ferdinando and Giuseppe Ruggeri around 1740 (the wooden model is on display in

*Above left:
the imposing dome of
the Chapel of the Princes*

*right:
Ferdinando and
Giuseppe Ruggeri
Wooden model for the
completion of the dome
in the Chapel of
the Princes*

*Below:
the crypt housing the
remains of the Medici
grandukes*

*Pages 138-139:
Michelangelo
Tomb of Lorenzo, duke
of Urbino:* Dawn
New Sacristy

*Facing page:
the opulent interior of
the Chapel of the Princes*

Spain, lapis lazuli, emeralds, topazes, agates, and amethysts were used to line the walls and decorate the frieze with the sixteen coats of arms of the cities of the grand duchy that runs along the whole of the tall plinth. Above it are set the six magnificent porphyry cenotaphs of the Medici grand dukes, two of them surmounted by imposing statues in gilded bronze. These are the work of Ferdinando and Pietro Tacca and depict Ferdinando I and Cosimo II in the dress of Knights of the Order of St. Stephen.

The initial design also called for the whole inside of the dome to be lined with coffers of lapis lazuli, adorned at the center with a rosette of gilded bronze. But the Medici never put this ambitious plan into effect and it was left to the house of Lorraine, their successors, to have it decorated. In 1828 they commissioned the painter Pietro Benvenuti from Arezzo to fresco the segments of the dome with scenes from the Old and New Testament and figures of Evangelists and Prophets. The work was completed in 1837. The original altar, designed by Buontalenti as a grandiose structure covered with semiprecious stones, was dismantled after 1728. The present

The Chapel of the Princes

The chapel is preceded by the crypt, a large space designed by Buontalenti and supported by squat and powerful pillars. Below it are located the Brunelleschian vaults of San Lorenzo (brought back to light and restored after the flood of 1966), where Cosimo the Elder and Donatello are buried. In 1858 Leopoldo II of Lorraine had the crypt renovated, with the installation of small tribunes on the walls, each intended to house the mortal remains of a grand duke, and slabs of marble commemorating other members of the Medici family in the floor, thereby putting an end to the practice of burying the dead underneath the paving.

Two flights of stairs lead to the Chapel of the Princes, a large and tall octagonal space dominated by the colors and opulence of the marble with which it is lined. The construction of this sumptuous building,

which according to a local tradition was intended to house the Holy Sepulcher after its transfer from Jerusalem to Florence, had already been planned by Cosimo I, even though work did not get under way until 1604, during the reign of his son Ferdinando I. The grand undertaking of its decoration was to keep the Opificio delle Pietre Dure, or Semiprecious Stone Works, busy for three centuries and required the outlay of huge sums of money, especially for the purchase of the stones. The enormous expenditure of energy and flaunting of great wealth had the sole purpose of arousing "wonder" in the Medici's visitors and respect in their subjects and the chapel became a great source of pride for the dukes. Notwithstanding its mortuary function, they used it to hold weddings and religious festivals and received delegations of foreign royalty there with great pomp.

Granite from Corsica and Egypt, violet marble from Flanders and coralline marble from

*Giuseppe Antonio
Torricelli
Reliquiary of
Saint Emeric*

*Below:
Giovan Battista Foggini
(design) and Giuseppe
Antonio Torricelli
(execution)
Reliquiary of
Saint Ambrose*

*Page 142 top:
the octagonal dome with
frescoes by Pietro
Benvenuti representing
scenes from the Old and
New Testament*

*below:
a silver crosier made
in Rome, a gift of
Pope Leo X*

one is the fruit of a reconstruction carried out in 1937, when panels inlaid with semiprecious stones or carved in relief from different periods were assembled and set in a wooden structure painted to resemble porphyry.

Reliquaries and liturgical objects donated to the church of San Lorenzo by the Medici over the centuries are displayed in two small spaces behind the altar. They include precious reliquaries from the seventeenth century (some made to designs by Giovan Battista Foggini and Massimiliano Soldani Benzi), the crosier, miter, and lectern cloths of Leo X, and more vessels for relics made of rock crystal, amethyst, and jasper, mostly from the Hellenistic and Roman periods, which used to belong to Lorenzo the Magnificent. The floor of the chapel, in green marble from Corsica and decorated with the Medici coat of arms, was not completed until 1962.

*Above:
Two of the twelve civic
coats of arms which
decorate the Chapel of
the Princes*

The New Sacristy

The design of the New Sacristy was commissioned from Michelangelo by Pope Leo X around 1520, as if to compensate him for having to cease work on the church's facade, on which the artist had been working with great enthusiasm for four years. The description of the building as a sacristy is a wholly conventional one and derives from the building's perfect symmetry with Brunelleschi's sacristy, which clearly provided the inspiration for the definition of the space inside as well. In fact the small room's function was, from the outset, that of a family chapel, in which Leo X wanted to honor the memory of his father Lorenzo the Magnificent and his uncle Giuliano, father of his cousin Giulio who was to succeed him on the papal throne under the name of Clemens VII. In addition, he wanted to commemorate Duke Lorenzo of Urbino and Duke Giuliano of Nemours, nephew and third son of Lorenzo the Magnificent respectively, who had been the first members of the family to gain a noble title.

The work, which commenced in 1521, went through a series of hiccups: the death of Leo X that same year brought the first interruption; the election of a new Medici pope, Clemens VII, two years later gave a new impetus to the work. In 1527 the Sack of Rome and the establishment of the Florentine Republic, which Michelangelo strongly supported, brought construction to a halt again and, on the death of Clemens VII in 1534, it was abandoned entirely, partly as a consequence of the artist's ever longer stays in Rome. Long left incomplete and with no statues, the chapel

was finally decorated by Vasari in 1555, at the behest of Cosimo I. The interior is a clear homage to Brunelleschi, although instead of the harmony and lucidity of the early fifteenth century, what we find here is an example of Michelangelo's desire to assign architecture and space not so much a structural function as a highly dramatic plastic effect, most evident in the dome and the walls with their continual projections and indentations. For the tombs, the artist had initially designed a single square monument, isolated at the center, with one sarcophagus set against each side. But when

Clemens VII expressed dissatisfaction with this arrangement, Michelangelo came up with four separate tombs set against the walls, blending in closely with the sculptural-architectural decoration of the chapel. One was intended for Duke Lorenzo of Urbino, another for Duke Giuliano of Nemours, and the last two for Lorenzo the Magnificent and his brother Giuliano, though these were never built. The small rectangular apse contains a Crucifix attributed to Giambologna and has two small chambers at the sides, known as *lavamani* (washstands). The one on the left leads to a

vault in which, during maintenance work carried out in 1975, a number of charcoal drawings in the style of Michelangelo were discovered on the walls. Some critics attribute them to Michelangelo himself, arguing that he drew them in the period between August and September of 1530 when, with the fall of the Florentine Republic and the return of the Medici to power, he went into hiding with the help of Giovanni Battista Figiovanni, superintendent of the works on the New Sacristy, who may have concealed him in this very cellar.

Michelangelo
Tomb of Lorenzo,
Duke of Urbino

Left:
view of the New Sacristy

Tomb of Duke Lorenzo of Urbino

The Duke of Urbino, to whom Niccolò Machiavelli had dedicated the *Prince*, is represented in an attitude of deep thought. An embodiment, therefore, of his reflective and cautious temperament, as described in the neoplatonic doctrines from which Michelangelo drew his inspiration. Dressed as a military leader, the young man is wearing a helmet with the mask of a lion on his head, perhaps a symbol of strength, while the small casket on which one elbow rests is probably a reference to thrift.

Allegories of *Dusk* and *Dawn* recline languidly on the sarcophagus below, in poses inspired by ancient statues of river gods.

Tomb of Duke Giuliano of Nemours

The third son of Lorenzo the Magnificent, who met a premature death in 1516, is also represented ideally as a military leader and, though seated, conveys a remarkable sense of energy through the marked torsion of his bust and head. The staff across his knees alludes to the Church, while the coin in his hand is a

symbol of generosity. In contrast to the duke of Urbino, Giuliano embodies energy, action, and resolute courage.

Allegories of *Night* and *Day* lie on the sarcophagus. Together with those of *Dusk* and *Dawn* on the tomb opposite, these symbolize the passing of time, which devours all.

The *Night*, one of the most famous sculptures of all time, is another expression of Michelangelo's ideal of female beauty, characterized by a powerful physique and a gaze of great tenderness. The attributes that

Michelangelo
Tomb of Giuliano,
Duke of Nemours

accompany the figure have been given various interpretations: the horrifying mask may be an allusion to nightmares and the bunch of poppies and the owl, references to sleep. In the *Day*, whose face has been carved with point and notched chisels, making it gleam in the light, we find once again Michelangelo's propensity for a strongly pictorial approach to sculpture.

The Madonna and Child with Saints Cosmas and Damian

Set on top of the bare coffin to which the remains of Lorenzo the Magnificent and his brother Giuliano were only transferred in 1559, the group of the *Madonna and Child* seems to have engaged Michelangelo's attention right from the start of his work on the chapel. Moreover the artist had already tackled the theme of the Madonna nursing the Child in several beautiful drawings he made between 1503 and 1504. In this sculpture he returned to it with renewed tenderness, although there is also a foreboding of sorrow and anxiety in the Virgin's intense expression and the uneasy composition. The most common view is that this sculpture forms the spiritual fulcrum of the entire chapel: in fact Giuliano and Lorenzo are gazing toward her, as if hoping to find in her a promise of redemption from the inexorable human destiny of death, to which the allegories on the sarcophagi allude.

Alongside the Virgin stand the statues of *Cosmas* and *Damian*, patron saints of the Medici family, carved by Giovannangelo da Montorsoli and Raffaello da Montelupo, artists in Michelangelo's circle.

Michelangelo
Madonna and Child

Page 148:
Michelangelo
Tomb of Giuliano, Duke
of Nemours: Day

PALAZZO PITTI

I t seems that Eleonora of Toledo was responsible for Palazzo Pitti becoming a residence of the Medici family. It is said that the consort of Cosimo I and daughter of the viceroy of Naples, accustomed to that city's sweeping views of the sea and the surrounding countryside, was greatly oppressed by the enclosed and fairly dark rooms of her new home in the "medieval" Palazzo Vecchio, where Cosimo had decided to move from the Palazzo Medici on via Larga. Apparently the duchess insisted on the purchase (in 1550) of the palace that Luca Pitti, a Florentine banker, had had built a century earlier (1443) on the Boboli hill. It is traditionally held to have been designed by Brunelleschi, a claim first made by Vasari, but it is more likely to have been the work of one of his pupils, Luca Fancelli. At the time the palace took the form of a regular parallelepiped. There were three portals and two rows of seven windows in its facade, i.e. the central part of the present building that faces onto the terraced square. Its current appearance dates from the eighteenth century and it has recently been subjected to extensive restoration, which has given the imposing structure back all of its fascination. The Medici grand duke and duchess wanted to turn it into an unusual kind of

classical tradition are blended with the liveliness of certain Mannerist ideas (such as the alternating bands of rustication on the upper stories). The courtyard itself, conceived as an extension of the architecture into the garden, served as a link between the latter and the palace. Thus the garden was turned into something like a piece of theatrical scenery, especially when the portals were hermetically sealed and the court, filled with water like a swimming pool, was used as the location for

residence that would be able to combine the formality of the townhouse with the comforts of a villa in the country: on the side of the hill, in fact, it opens onto the magnificent Boboli Gardens that were being laid out at the same time. They entrusted the completion of the work to Bartolomeo Ammannati. He made changes to the facade, removing the two doorways at the sides and replacing them with windows with outward curving bars, derived from the architecture of Michelangelo, and to the rear, creating the great inner court in the Renaissance manner, in which elements drawn from the

unusual spectacles and mock naval battles, during ceremonies that the grand duke and duchess and their guests watched from the terrace that runs along the second floor.

At the same time another important idea took shape: the Corridoio Vasariano, named after its creator, which formed a direct link between the "country" palace and the city one, through a sort of covered gallery that ran from the Palazzo Vecchio, through the Uffizi and across the

Orazio Scarabelli
Naval Battle
*Uffizi, Gabinetto
Disegni e Stampe*

*Above:
the facade of Palazzo
Pitti today*

*Below:
Bernardo Buontalenti
engraving showing*
Palazzo Pitti
*Uffizi, Gabinetto
Disegni e Stampe*

grottoes. And some of the most refined and spectacular of these additions were the product of Buontalenti's genius, including the remarkable grotto named after him, used as the exit to the Corridoio Vasariano. An example of the most lively Florentine Mannerism, it is decorated inside with a variety of materials (shells, sponges, terra-cottas) in a highly original way. Water used to flow between the decorations through complicated devices invented by Buontalenti himself which earned him the epithet "engineer of gardens." However, the work on enlargement of the palace did not come to an end with Ammannati's interventions, but continued the following century, when the architects Giulio and Alfonso Parigi added a double row of eight windows on each side along the lines of the original Brunelleschian design, with very homogeneous results. The two lateral wings that form the terrace, on the other hand, date from the Lorraine period and were built by Giuseppe Ruggeri and Gaspare Maria

Ponte Vecchio, to the Pitti residence. A few decades later, the gifted architect Bernardo Buontalenti was commissioned by Ferdinando I to erect a fortification on the top of the hill (1590-95). This was the Belvedere Fort, intended to protect the palace and garden, which in the meantime had begun to change its appearance, with the erection of fountains, statues, and

Boboli Garden,
the Isolotto pond

Above:
the courtyard of Palazzo
Pitti designed by
Bartolomeo Ammannati

Below:
Boboli Garden, front
of the Grotto of
Buontalenti

Pages 150-151:
Justus Utens
lunette with the
Belvedere and Palazzo
Pitti, *detail*
Museo di Firenze
com'era

Paoletti. The latter was also responsible, along with Pasquale Poccianti, for the later construction of the Palazzina della Meridiana, at the southern end of the whole complex. The embellishment of the interiors went hand in hand with the work on the exterior, especially after the Medici family moved permanently into the palace. In particular the grand duke's rooms on the *piano nobile* which face onto the square, known as the "winter apartment" (and now housing the Palatine Gallery), and the rooms in the north wing of the ground floor underneath (part of what is now the Museum of Silverware), were decorated with magnificent cycles of paintings by Pietro da Cortona, Giovanni da San Giovanni, Angelo Michele Colonna, and Agostino Mitelli. These are still the finest examples of baroque art in Florence. Yet interventions of high quality were made in every century in which the palace was inhabited – right up to the time when it was briefly the king's residence during the years that Florence was the capital of Italy (1865-71). These reflect the tastes of the time and the personalities of the city's rulers and increase the fascination of a building so filled with history, and one that with the recent works of restoration, reorganization, and adaptation is also one of the richest and best preserved museum complexes in Italy.

The Palatine Gallery

Among the numerous collections of figurative and applied arts housed within the palace's sober architecture (Royal Apartments, Museum of Silverware, Gallery of Modern Art, Costume Gallery, Porcelain Museum, Carriage Museum), the Palatine Gallery is certainly the most famous and frequently visited. This may be partly due to its character as an intact

*The Sala di Giovanni
da San Giovanni
Museo degli Argenti*

*Below:
the Sala della Stufa
Galleria Palatina*

princely collection of paintings. It occupies the left-hand wing of the palace's *piano nobile*, to which access is provided by Ammannati's broad staircase, and much of it is decorated with frescoes in the baroque style. It was Vittoria della Rovere and her consort, Grand Duke Ferdinando II de' Medici, who entrusted the decoration of the small "Stanza della Stufa" to Pietro da Cortona, whose exuberant style had already been used to decorate churches and palaces in Rome. The perfect execution of the *Four Ages of Man* (1637-40), in light and vivid colors, provided ample proof of the artist's skill and induced the grand duke to extend the commission to the rooms at the front of the palace, which were used for political and social receptions. The ceilings, decorated by Pietro and completed by his pu-

pil Ciro Ferri, were devoted to the glorification of the Medici family – through the allegorical representation of the planets discovered by Galileo under Medici patronage and through allegories and metaphors drawing on mythical and historical events – in *trompe-l'oeil* perspective vibrant with movement and illusionistic exchanges between the stuccowork, itself very beautiful, and the painting. This lavish decoration, perhaps the most splendid example of the baroque in Florence, extends to the furnishings and the walls, which are covered with masterpieces of Italian and foreign painting from the Renaissance to the seventeenth century. Yet it is far more difficult to appreciate the individual qualities of the works on these overcrowded walls than it is in the Uffizi, where the pictures are arranged in chronological order and according to didactic principles. The Palatine Gallery is a rare example of a princely collection preserved in its original form, where the beautiful paintings are displayed in lavish frames and amidst refined tapestries and furnishings, arranged solely on the principle of the elegance of the overall effect.

So there can be no doubt that the Palatine Gallery presents considerable difficulties for the modern tourist. Rather than treating the museum as an educational experience, visitors should allow themselves to be guided by the fascinating uniqueness of the historical assemblage. It is an expression of the sensitivity and

The Sala di Prometeo
Galleria Palatina

taste of first the Medici family and then the house of Lorraine, who filled these rooms with works of great value with the sole aim of the family's private enjoyment. The first nucleus of the works now on show in the gallery was assembled by Cosimo II de' Medici (1620). Subsequent additions were made by Ferdinando II and Cosimo III, and the collection was further enlarged by Pietro Leopoldo of Lorraine, though he too maintained the private character of the apartments. It attained its definitive form, however, toward the end of the eighteenth century, through the efforts of Ferdinando II and Leopoldo II. It was officially opened to a select public in 1833, five years after the first catalogue had been printed and at a time when several rooms had assumed a modern appearance, with decorations, stuccoes, and furniture in the Empire style.

The Sala di Venere
Galleria Palatina

Tiziano Vecellio, called **Titian**
(Pieve di Cadore 1490? – Venice 1576)
■ *The Concert*
Sala di Venere
canvas, 86.5x123.5 cm
The painting was acquired in Venice by
Cardinal Leopoldo de' Medici, in 1654, as a
work by Giorgione. Its beauty earned it a
place in the Tribuna at the Uffizi, until it was
transferred to Palazzo Pitti in 1697, at the
behest of Grand Prince Ferdinando. Today
critics are almost unanimous in assigning it to
the young Titian (1510/12), at a time when
he was evidently still under the influence of
his teacher Giorgione. It is not clear what
subject the picture represents: it is generally
thought to be a concert, and it is clear that
music is the central theme, but other
meanings could be attached to the three male
figures, which may be a sort of representation
of the three ages of man similar to the
painting by Giorgione in the nearby Sala di
Giove.

Titian
■ *Portrait of Pietro Aretino*
Sala di Venere
canvas, 96.7x76.6 cm
The picture arrived in Florence the year it was
painted, 1545, as a gift to Cosimo II from
Aretino himself. The Tuscan man of letters lived
in Venice and was a close friend of Titian's. The
artist has brought out the disquieting character
of his subject, whose writings were greatly
feared at European courts for their
ferociously satirical and provocative content.

Even here Aretino did not fail to live up to his
reputation, claiming that the portrait was not
finished because the artist had not been paid
enough. However, he tempered this judgment
by admitting that the portrait "[...] breathes,
pulsates, and moves the spirit in the way that I
do in life."

Titian
■ *Portrait of a Lady*, known as *La Bella*
Sala di Venere
canvas, 89x75.5 cm
This celebrated picture depicts an unknown
lady whose resemblance to the *Venus of Urbino*
in the Uffizi has led critics from the eighteenth
century onward to believe that she was Titian's
mistress. The portrait is of high quality: the
woman's gaze is intense and the depiction of
her elegant dress – finely decorated with gold
embroidery and showing white puffs through
the luxurious velvet sleeves – is extremely
accurate. We know that the picture cannot
have been painted later than 1537 from a
letter written by the duke of Urbino to the
artist in Venice in that year, asking for news of
the portrait of a lady in blue that Titian was
supposed to have sent him. The picture came
to Florence as part of the dowry of Vittoria
della Rovere, who married Grand Duke
Ferdinando II in 1631.

Titian
- *Portrait of a Man with Gray Eyes*
Sala di Apollo
canvas, 111x96 cm

The Sala di Apollo houses two more famous works by Titian – *The Repentant Magdalen* and this *Portrait of a Man* – showing why this artist is considered one of the gallery's great sources of pride. All attempts to identify the young man have proved vain. The figure stands out delicately from the dark background, rendered with skillful strokes of the brush and ever so slightly brightened up at the neck and sleeves by the white lace of his shirt. Another element that confirms the exceptional quality of this portrait from Titian's early maturity (ca. 1545), mentioned as belonging to the collections of the grand dukes of Florence from 1698 onward, is provided by those gray-green and transparent eyes with their look of great psychological penetration. The title of the "Young Englishman" by which it is known was given to the portrait in the nineteenth century.

Andrea del Sarto (Florence 1486 – 1530)
- *Luco Pietà*
Sala di Apollo
panel, 238x198 cm

The Sala di Apollo houses several masterpieces of early sixteenth-century Florentine painting, such as this *Luco Pietà*. Known by this name because it was painted for the church of San Pietro a

Luco, in Mugello, it is a very fine example of Florentine Mannerist coloring, influenced by the Roman work of Michelangelo and Raphael. The composition of the altarpiece is clearly based on the one by Fra Bartolomeo in the nearby Sala di Giove, but the bold use of color and the more energetic and complex treatment of the volumes of the figures lend a grandeur to the whole that is foreign to the work of Fra Bartolomeo and closer to that of Michelangelo.

Giovan Battista di Jacopo, called **Rosso Fiorentino**
(Florence 1495 – Fontainebleau 1540)
- *Virgin Enthroned with Saints*
Sala di Apollo
panel, 350x259 cm

Also known as the *Dei Altarpiece*, it comes from the chapel of that name in Santo Spirito, for which it was painted in 1522. It entered the collection of Grand Prince Ferdinando at the end of the seventeenth century, when he decided he wanted the painting in Palazzo Pitti. It was at this time that the obvious

enlargement of the panel was carried out, so that it would fit into a sumptuous baroque frame. The daring choice of shades of color and the troubled expressions of the figures are typical of the tone preferred by an artist who has often been considered bizarre.

Pieter Paul Rubens
(Siegen 1577 – Antwerp 1640)
■ *The Four Philosophers*
Sala di Marte
panel, 164x139 cm

The oldest and most elegantly dressed figure at the center of the symposium can be identified as a Dutch Humanist philosopher, Justus Lipsius, teacher of the artist's brother, who is also portrayed on the left, with Rubens himself beyond him. The man seated on the right is another of Lipsius's pupils, Jean van de Wouwère. Keeping vigil over the conversation is the sculpted image of Seneca – copied from the bust that Rubens acquired in Rome in 1605 – which has given rise to Stoic interpretations of the picture as an extolling of moral virtues over the corrupt customs of the time. When Rubens painted this scene at Antwerp in 1611-12, his brother Philip and his teacher had already died. It is argued by some that, in keeping with the taste for symbolic representation typical of European culture, the four figures in the picture can be identified with the tulips set alongside Seneca: a homage to the great philosopher by the two living men (the flowers still in bud) and the two dead men (the two flowers that have already faded). The bright tones of color testify to the influence of the Venetian painting Rubens admired and studied on his visit to Italy.

Bartolomé Esteban Murillo
(Seville 1618 – 1682)
■ *Madonna and Child*
Sala di Marte
canvas, 157x107 cm
This work is typical of the artist from Seville, famous for the religious intensity of his pictures of the *Madonna and Child*. An atmosphere rich in sentiment and color is combined with a realistic characterization of the figures, as was the custom in seventeenth-century Spanish art. The provenance of the picture in the Medici collections is not known. It is the companion to another, similar but less well-known painting called the *Madonna of the Rosary*, both of them early works from around 1650.

Pieter Paul Rubens
■ *The Consequences of War*
Sala di Marte
canvas, 206x345 cm
Two different views of war are represented in the Sala di Marte: a triumphal one intended to celebrate the martial prowess and victories of the Medici family, painted with masterly skill on the ceiling by Pietro da Cortona, and an allegorical one by Rubens, who in his bombastic manner wished to issue a warning about the tragic circumstances and disastrous consequences

of war. Rubens himself, in the letter that accompanied the picture when he sent it in 1638 to Justus Sustermans, the court painter in Florence, explains that the woman with the broken lute – in the foreground on the right of the canvas – represents shattered harmony, and that fecundity, civilization, and the arts (represented by other figures in the picture) are swept away by war, to which the open doors of the temple of Janus also allude. The richly colored and deeply cadenced painting matches the subject, with its many

figures and strong sentiments. It is a picture that conveys the anguish felt by Rubens during the years of civil war in Flanders.

Paolo Caliari, called **Veronese**
(Verona 1528 – Venice 1588)
■ *Portrait of a Man*
Sala di Marte
canvas, 140x107 cm
Like Titian's *Concert*, the portrait was acquired by Cardinal Leopoldo de' Medici's envoy in Venice, Paolo del Sera, in 1659.

The gentleman is portrayed in a majestic pose and dressed in a splendid lynx fur. The picture was painted by Veronese, between 1550 and 1560, with great freedom and fluency and is reminiscent of Titian's portraiture. The Venetian nobleman has long been thought to be the Humanist Daniele Barbaro.

Jacopo Robusti, called **Tintoretto**
(Venice 1518 – 1594)
■ *Portrait of Alvise Cornaro*
Sala di Marte
canvas, 113x85 cm
The date of the picture can be deduced from the venerable age of the Venetian Humanist and patron of the arts, portrayed shortly before his death in 1566 at the age of ninety-one. It is a fine example of Tintoretto's use of dark tones set off by warm patches of color. The work must have been a particular favorite of Grand Prince Ferdinando, who kept it in his bedchamber in the grand ducal apartments.

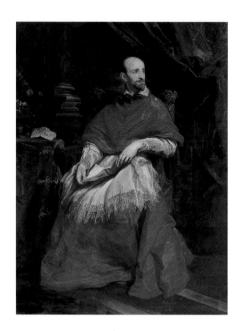

Anton van Dyck

(Antwerp 1599 – London 1641)

■ *Portrait of Cardinal Bentivoglio*

Sala di Marte

canvas, 195x147 cm

At the time of this portrait (1622-23), one of van Dyck's masterpieces, Giudo Bentivoglio had just been appointed cardinal ambassador of the pope in Flanders. In this picture the artist combines the characteristic fluidity he had imbibed from Venetian coloring, amply displayed in the red robes worn by the cardinal and the velvet drapes in the background, with a studied and realistic representation of the details derived from the Flemish tradition. The monumentality of the picture, justified by the high status of the subject, author of a famous *History of the Wars in Flanders*, is reminiscent of the official portraiture of Raphael, by that time a celebrated model and certainly known to the Flemish painter.

Giorgio Zorzi, called **Giorgione**

(Castelfranco Veneto 1477/78 – Venice 1510)

■ *The Three Ages of Man*

Sala di Giove

panel, 62x77 cm

The recent restoration (1987) has provided confirmation of the attribution of this picture to Giorgione. It has been recognized as one of the paintings by the Venetian master that used to belong to the Vendramin collection in 1567, and which was later bought in Venice on behalf of Grand Prince Ferdinando.

The three figures, perhaps engaged in a singing lesson, stand out from the monochromatic darkness of the background with a delicacy of tonal and atmospheric gradations that is reminiscent of Leonardo. In the sixteenth and seventeenth century there was a great passion for chamber music concerts in the Humanistic circles that Giorgione frequented in Venice, and in fact his love of music and poetry is also recorded by the old sources.

Florentine painting of the early sixteenth century. The picture was probably painted in 1523 for the antechamber of the palace of Giovan Maria Benintendi, who later donated it to Cosimo I.

Bartolomeo della Porta, called **Fra Bartolomeo** (Florence 1472 – 1517)
■ *Lamentation over the Dead Christ*
Sala di Giove
panel, 158x199 cm
The long work of restoration to which the painting was subjected a decade ago (1985-88) has brought to light the original background, i.e. the landscape behind the irremediably mutilated figures of St. Peter and St. Paul in the upper part.
The reduction in size of the work probably dates from the time of its acquisition by Cardinal Carlo de' Medici, in 1619, and was a consequence of the baroque fashion for dark backgrounds and the needs of its private owner, who wanted the picture to fit into a smaller frame than the original. Today, the *Lamentation* once again displays the brilliant colors typical of this painter, who was a forerunner of Mannerist coloring, and this makes possible a fairer evaluation of the construction of the figures in space.

Andrea del Sarto
■ *The Young Saint John*
Sala di Giove
panel, 94x68 cm
This is one of the finest paintings from the maturity of Andrea del Sarto, an artist who is particularly well represented in the gallery, with a total of sixteen works.
The image of Saint John presented by Andrea is a very intense one: heroic, with a proud and ardent gaze that blends classicism with the expressive disquiet of the

Raffaello Sanzio, called **Raphael**
(Urbino 1483 – Rome 1520)
■ *Portrait of a Woman* or *The Woman in a Veil*
Sala di Giove
canvas, 82x60.5 cm
This is the most famous painting in the Sala di Giove. Its unknown subject, portrayed with consummate mastery, is traditionally held to be the artist's beloved, the celebrated "Fornarina" mentioned by Vasari. In fact she greatly resembles the woman in the similar portrait (*Portrait of Fornarina*) in Palazzo Barberini in Rome. The figure displays a number of delicate touches, such as the unruly lock of hair and the softness of the clothes, that make it one of Raphael's finest paintings, although it is only in this century that it has been reassigned to him after a long period in which it was not thought to be his own work. Dating from late in his career, around 1516, it entered the grand ducal collections in 1622, acquired from its previous owners, the Botti family.

Raphael
■ *Madonna del Granduca*
Sala di Saturno
panel, 84.5x55.9 cm
This elegant *Madonna and Child* set against a darkened background, like those of Leonardo's paintings, derives its name (the *Grand Duke's Madonna*) from the Lorraine family's attachment to the picture. In fact it was acquired by Ferdinando III at the end of the eighteenth century, during his exile in Vienna, and from then on the grand duke always kept it in his private apartments. So the picture only became known through the engravings and prints that the Lorraine had made of it, and was not seen by the public until the opening of the Palatine Gallery. The radiographs taken during its restoration have revealed a window under the dark ground: thus it probably had a domestic setting suited, along with its small size, to the needs of a private client.

Raphael
■ *Tommaso Inghirami*, called *Fedra*
Sala di Saturno
panel, 89.5x62 cm
Yet another painting by Raphael in the room in the Gallery that has the privilege of housing the largest group of his works. The artist knew this poet and orator from Volterra well. The portrait probably dates from 1510, the year in which he was appointed papal librarian by Leo X. So the painter must have felt free to show the obvious squint in his right eye without this detracting from the overall dignity of the figure. The classical pose of the subject, similar to that used for representations of the evangelists, combined with a mutability created by the subtle variations in the tones of red, opens a new phase in Raphael's portraiture, in which he was able to instill a sense of movement even into a formal portrait. Inghirami, educated at the court of Lorenzo the Magnificent, was a man of letters and the author of a play, *Fedra* (*Phaedra*), which earned him his curious nickname.

Raphael

■ *Portraits of Agnolo and Maddalena Doni*
Sala di Saturno
panels, 65x45.7 cm (each)
Agnolo Doni was a wealthy Florentine merchant who, at the time this diptych was painted, had already commissioned from Michelangelo the famous tondo depicting the *Holy Family*, now in the Uffizi. He married Maddalena Strozzi in 1503 while the portraits date from 1506-7, and were intended as a good omen for the birth of children, since monochromes alluding to fertility have been painted on the back of the two panels. These have been identified as the work of one of Raphael's collaborators, the Master of Serumido. Here Raphael seems to want to remind us of a masterly example of the double portrait, Piero della Francesca's *Duke and Duchess of Urbino*, adding subtleties in the handling of atmosphere and in the scenery in the background in which it is possible to detect the influence of Leonardo and of the landscapes dear to his teacher Perugino. The two pictures did not enter the grand ducal collections until 1826, when Leopoldo II bought them from the heirs of the Doni family on the advice of the French painter François Xavier Fabre.

Raphael

■ *Madonna della Seggiola*
Sala di Saturno
panel, diam. 71 cm
This is perhaps the most famous of Raphael's masterpieces, admired by all and endlessly copied. It is a perfect handling of the Florentine tradition of the tondo, used to present a masterly glimpse of domestic

life, intimate and lively in its dynamism and its balance of solids and voids. The unusual pose of the Madonna – to whom Raphael gives very human accouterments and features, behind which the face of his beloved Fornarina seems once again to be concealed – who is gently clasping the Child, imparts a circular movement to the composition and reveals the influence of Michelangelo.

Yet under this apparently modest appearance, which led to the picture being considered a portrait of a mother with her son in the nineteenth century, are concealed signs that it was in fact painted for a client of high rank: the length of silk cloth wound around her head like a turban in a Turkish fashion that was in vogue among women of the upper classes, and the chair in the foreground (from which the picture takes its name, the *Madonna of the Chair*) resembling those in use at the papal court. This has led to the suggestion of Leo X as a possible client, sometime around 1516.

Pietro Vannucci, called **Perugino**
(Città della Pieve ca. 1448 – Fontignano 1523)
■ *Lamentation over the Dead Christ*
Sala di Saturno
panel, 214x195 cm

This picture, with its complex composition and throng of figures in deeply reverent attitudes, became a source of inspiration for the artists of the sixteenth century. Perugino's student Raphael used it as a model for his *Deposition*, now in the Galleria Borghese in Rome, as did Fra Bartolomeo for his *Lamentation*, which can be seen in the nearby Sala di Giove.

It is signed and dated 1495, on the stone on which Christ's body is laid, and was painted for the former convent of Santa Chiara on via dei Serragli.

Artemisia Gentileschi
(Rome 1593 – Naples 1652)
■ *Judith with the Head of Holofernes*
Sala dell'Iliade
canvas, 117x93 cm

Together with many other works from the sixteenth and seventeenth centuries, this fine canvas by Artemisia Gentileschi hangs in the largest and most sumptuous room in the gallery, decorated (1819-25) by Luigi Sabatelli with scenes from the *Iliad*.

A painter of great intensity, Artemisia derived her use of strong chiaroscuro and realistic style from Caravaggio, who she came to know personally through her father Orazio. Yet she employed them in her own way to produce theatrical effects and convey the precious nature of the materials she represented. A disquieting figure, and one of the very few women to have earned a place in the history of art, she portrays here a subject that recurs frequently in her work.

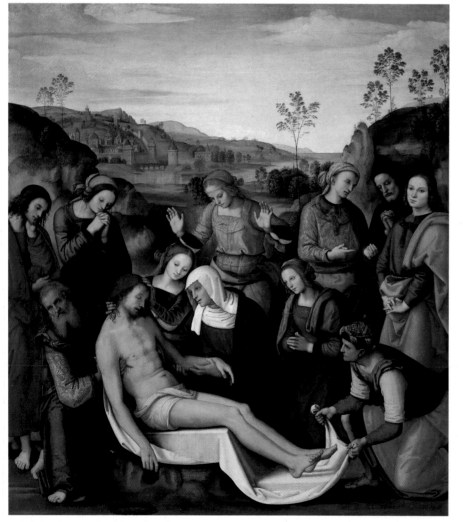

Michelangelo Merisi, called **Caravaggio** (Caravaggio or Milan 1570/71 – Porto Ercole 1610)
■ *Sleeping Cupid*
Sala dell'Educazione di Giove
canvas, 71x105 cm
Caravaggio painted this *Cupid* on Malta and sent it to the man who commissioned it, Niccolò dell'Antella, in Florence. The grazing angle of the light creates effects of surprising realism and imparts a different, unaccustomed tone to the classical representation of this subject. The painting was acquired by Cardinal Leopoldo de' Medici in 1667.

It must have been at this time that it was given the frame in which we see it today, on which a number of Cupid's iconographic attributes, such as the bow and arrows, are depicted.

Cristofano Allori (Florence 1577 – 1621)
■ *Judith with the Head of Holofernes*
Sala dell'Educazione di Giove
canvas, 139x116 cm
The popularity of this painting is demonstrated by the many reproductions that are known to have been made of it. In fact it is the masterpiece of this Florentine artist, whose mellow style and opaque colors reflect the influence of Correggio and the sixteenth-century artists of the Veneto region. The picture, mentioned in several literary works, was appreciated by his contemporaries for the beauty of Judith, which contrasts with the resolute gesture of the hand holding Holofernes's head. These figures can be identified as the painter himself and his favorite model, Mazzafirra.

Ludovico Cardi, called **Cigoli** (Castelvecchio di Cigoli, Florence, 1559 – Rome 1613)
■ *Ecce Homo*
Sala di Ulisse
canvas, 175x135 cm
This work was traditionally held to be the one that Cigoli entered, along with a number of other painters including Caravaggio and Passignano, for a competition held in Rome by Cardinal Massimi in 1606. Cigoli is supposed to have won the competition, but recent documentary finds seem to give the lie to this story told in the biography of the Tuscan artist written by his nephew Giovan Battista Cigoli, and throw more light on the chronology of the works involved in the affair. Cigoli's canvas can be dated to two years later (1607) than the one painted by Caravaggio in 1605 (now in the Museo di Palazzo Bianco at Genoa), and is therefore likely to have been derived from the picture by the seventeenth-century master of realism. The directed light, in the manner of Caravaggio, helps to augment the dramatic theatricality of the scene, along with details like the drops of blood running down the balustrade, creating an atmosphere of intense religious sentimentalism.

of the group in the foreground, arranged in an almost perfect circle. The little St. John, painted after various changes of mind that are testified by the drawing in the Uffizi and confirmed by radiography, concludes this rotary movement. The work was commissioned from Raphael in 1514 by Bindo Altoviti, a Florentine banker at the papal court.

Filippino Lippi
(Prato ca. 1457 – Florence 1504)
■ *The Death of Lucretia*
Sala di Ulisse
panel, 42x126 cm
The elongated shape of the panel is explained by the fact that it used to form the side of a wedding chest. The theme depicted, an exaltation of female virtue to its highest degree, is also suited to the picture's original function. According to the story related by Livy, Lucretia was driven to take her own life after being raped by Sextus Tarquinius, son of the king Tarquinius Superbus, spurring the Romans to revolt against the tyrant. In fact a quiver of rebellion runs through the groups of figures in Renaissance dress, conveyed by the fluttering drapery and their agitated movement against a backdrop of Renaissance buildings, with evident references to classical architecture. In this work dating from around 1470, Filippino's style is close to that of his friend Botticelli, who was later to paint a similar scene.

Raphael
■ *Madonna dell'impannata*
Sala di Ulisse
panel, 160x127 cm
One of the works most often reproduced by the followers of Raphael, it has been confidently reassigned to the master himself following the restoration carried out in the eighties, which has revealed the high quality of the painting. The name comes from the window in the background, covered with a piece of starched cloth called *impannata* to protect the room against the cold. This helps to give the picture a domestic tone that is only slightly attenuated by the refined composition

Jacopo Carrucci, called **Pontormo**
(Pontorme, Empoli, 1495 – Florence 1556)
■ *Adoration of the Magi*
Sala di Prometeo
panel, 85x191 cm
This picture, along with Andrea del Sarto's
Young Saint John and works by Franciabigio
and Granacci, used to decorate the
antechamber in the palace of Giovanni Maria
Benintendi. Like the other painting by the
artist in this room, the *Martyrdom of the
Eleven Thousand*, the *Adoration* shows clear
traces of the influence of Michelangelo in the
imposing and powerful frames of the figures,
often in strained poses. But his apprenticeship

with Andrea del Sarto led Pontormo to
develop a highly personal style that, through
distorted bodies and shimmering colors that
are far more daring and extravagant than
Michelangelo's, conveys the sense of a restless
psychological probing typical of the European
art of the early sixteenth century.

Sandro Filipepi, called **Botticelli**
(Florence 1445 – 1510)
■ *Portrait of a Young Man wearing
a Mazzocchio*
Sala di Prometeo
panel, 51x34 cm
While the painting has suffered badly from
restorations carried out in the past, the image
of the man dressed in a typical Renaissance
tunic and a *mazzocchio*, the fashionable
headgear made famous by Paolo Uccello's
representations of it in perspective, remains
quite clear. The attribution to Botticelli is still
uncertain. Its monumental and terse style have
led critics to put forward the name of an older
painter, Andrea del Castagno (which would
mean putting back the date of the picture), or
that of Piero di Cosimo.

Filippo Lippi

(Florence 1406 – Spoleto 1469)

■ *Madonna and Child and Birth of Mary*

Sala di Prometeo

panel, diam. 135 cm

The arrangement of the figures and scenes in this painting by Lippi is complex. It is the most important of the numerous tondi on show in the Sala di Prometeo. It looks almost as if the artist wanted to use the slight twisting of the figure of the Virgin in the foreground to establish a connection with the events taking place behind her. These, in turn, are laid out within a complex and precise perspective structure with several vanishing points and illusionistic spaces. On the left, the majority of the space is taken up by the *Birth of the Virgin Mary*, on the right by the *Meeting of Joachim and Saint Anna*. Stylistically, the lively decoration of the drapery in which the figures are cloaked suggests that this tondo, painted for an unknown client, dates from the time of the frescoes in Prato Cathedral (ca. 1450).

Titian

■ *Tommaso Mosti (?)*
Sala della Giustizia
canvas, 85x66 cm

The restoration carried out at the beginning of the century brought to light a seventeenth-century inscription on the back of the canvas that identifies the subject of the portrait as Tommaso Mosti – a Ferrarese man of letters, aged twenty-five at the time – and allows the painting to be dated to 1526. Yet there are a number of inconsistencies with the historical records, even though the dating of the picture seems plausible in relation to the artist's style. Thus it has been suggested that the subject is not Tommaso Mosti, but his brother Vincenzo, a close friend of Duke Alfonso d'Este, whose portrait Titian is believed to have painted around 1520.

Andrea del Sarto

■ *Scenes from the Life of the Patriarch Joseph*
Sala di Flora
panels, 98x135 cm (each)

These two panel paintings by Andrea del Sarto were part of the cycle that Pier Francesco Borgherini had commissioned to decorate his nuptial chamber. This room must have contained an impressive selection of early sixteenth-century Florentine painting, as Andrea's pictures were accompanied by works by Bachiacca, Pontormo, and Granacci. Later the decoration was dismembered and the panels in question were bought by Grand Duke Francesco I, who placed them in the Tribuna of the Uffizi. Among the artist's finest works, they illustrate in brilliant tones of color the story of Joseph son of Jacob, who is set free by the pharaoh as a reward for his skill at the interpretation of dreams.

Baldassare Franceschini, called
Volterrano (Volterra 1611 – Florence 1690)
■ *Arlotto's Trick*
Sala delle Allegorie
canvas, 107x150 cm
This celebrated picture by the Tuscan artist is
an example of the humorous genre that arose
out of the tradition of popular literature. It
depicts the trick played with wine by the
parish priest Arlotto Mainardi – who actually
existed, and was famous for his jokes – and is
set under the portico of the Villa della Mula at
Quinto, near Florence. The atmosphere of
gaiety is conveyed through the use of light,
airy colors, combined with a sketchy style.
The painting was commissioned by Francesco
Parrocchiani and sold by him to Cardinal
Giovan Carlo de' Medici thirty years later
(1670).

Rachel Ruysch (Amsterdam 1664 – 1750)
■ *Still Life with Flowers, Fruit, and Insects*
Sala dei Putti
canvas, 89x69 cm
With the two canvases by Rachel Ruysch,
the Sala dei Putti offers a foretaste of the
wonderful collection of still lifes in the Palazzo
Pitti – a tangible demonstration of the refined
taste of the Medici – and partly on show in

the Quartiere del Volterrano. Both were
purchased by Ferdinando III and are signed
and dated 1716. This *Still Life with Flowers,
Fruit, and Insects* is an elegant example of the
Flemish genre of still life, meticulously
reproduced down to the tiniest detail and
made up of the most varied types of fruit.
Natural objects studied with almost scientific
precision by a painter who must have been
influenced by the profession of her father, a
student of anatomy and botany.

INDEX OF ARTISTS

© 1997 SCALA, Istituto Fotografico Editoriale, Antella
and Editrice Giusti di Becocci e C., Florence

Layout: Matilde Contri
Translation: Christopher Evans
Editing: Marilena Vecchi
Photographic acknowledgements: SCALA ARCHIVE
(M. Falsini, M. Sarri) except for p. 68 (property of
the Cassa di Risparmio di Firenze S.p.A.)
Printed in Italy by Arti Grafiche "Stampa Nazionale",
Calenzano (Florence), 1999